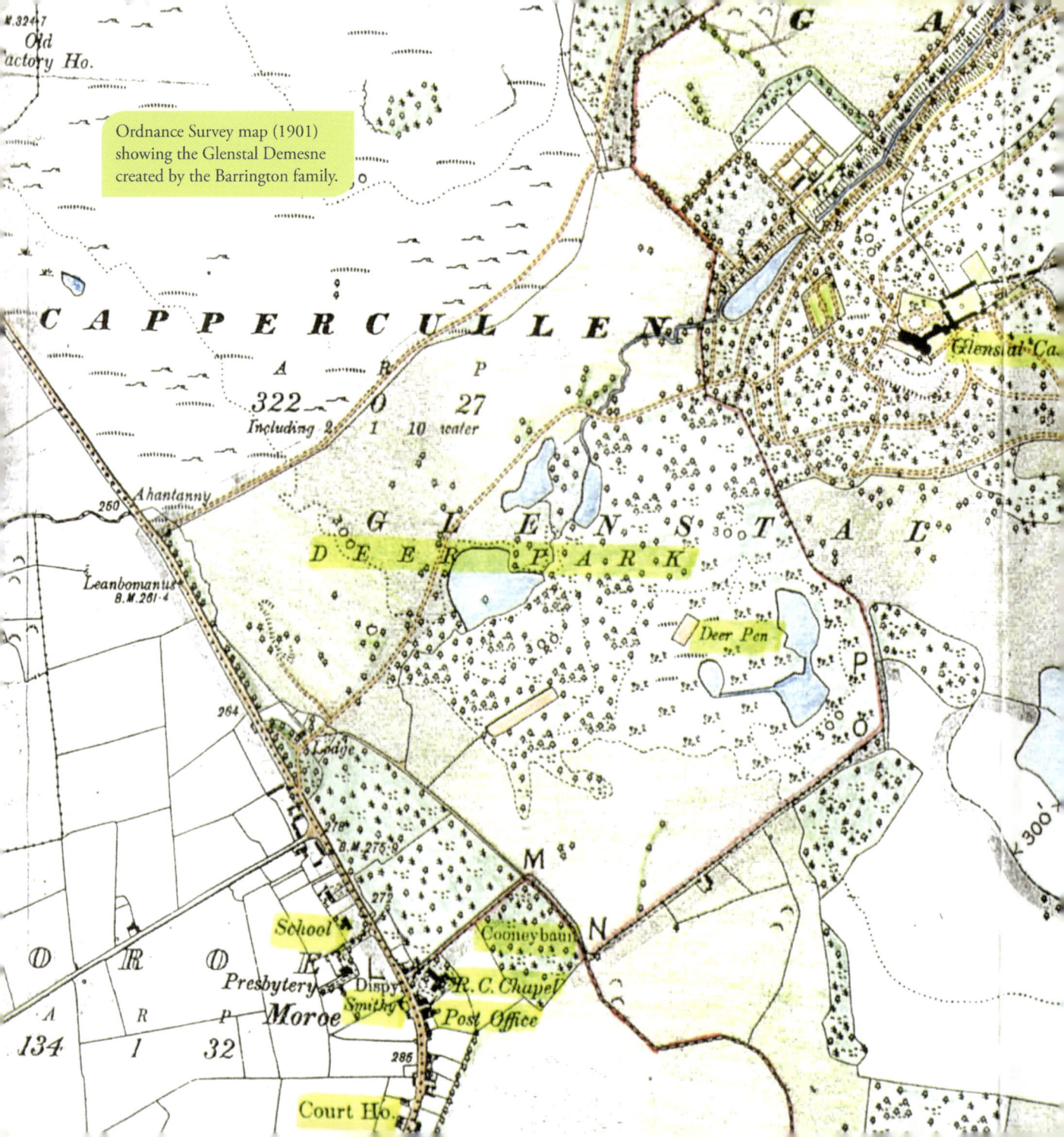
Ordnance Survey map (1901) showing the Glenstal Demesne created by the Barrington family.

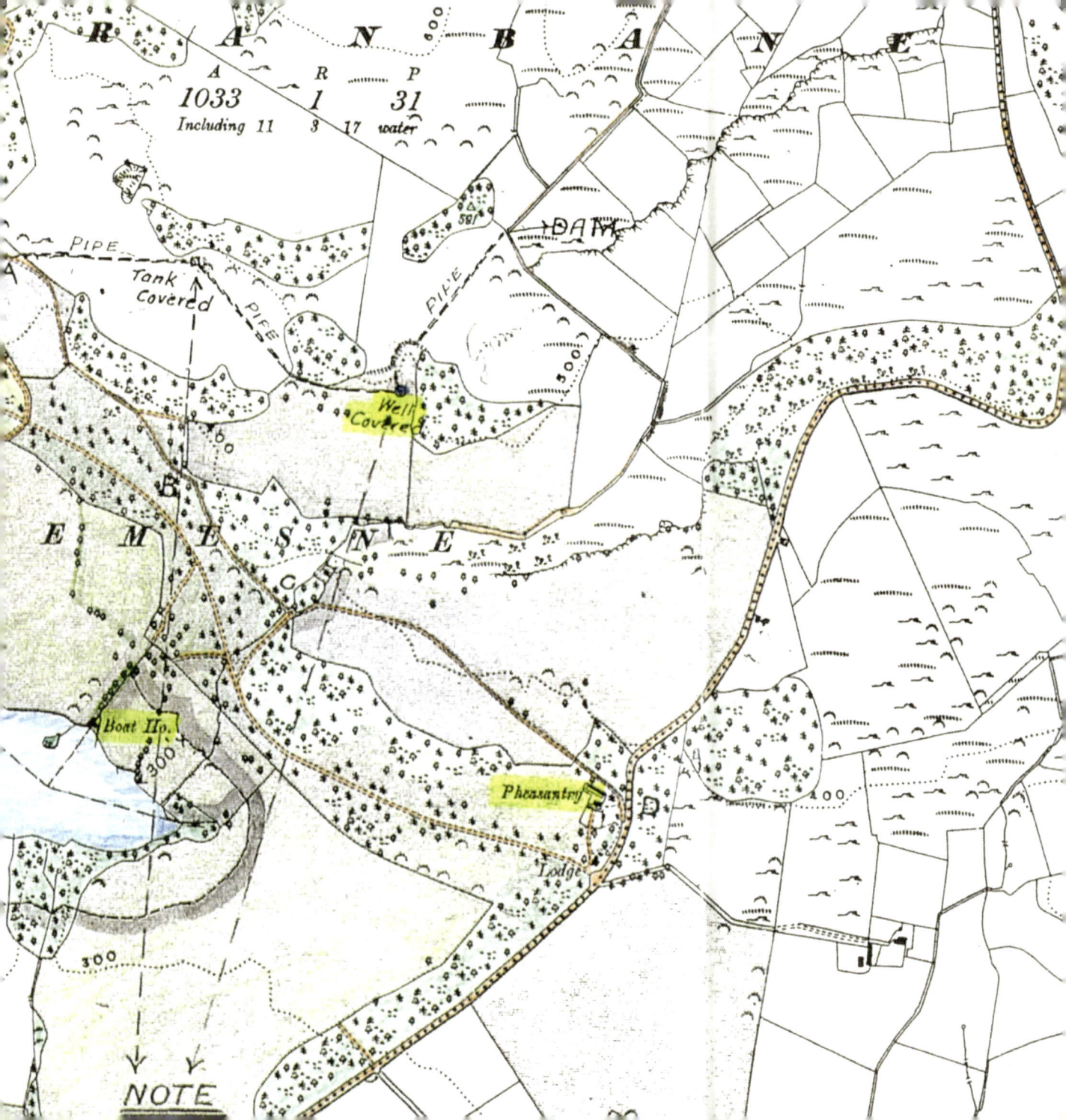

GLENSTAL ABBEY GARDENS

C. 1650 TO THE PRESENT:
FROM TOWNLAND TO TERRACE GARDEN AND BEYOND

GLENSTAL ABBEY GARDENS

C. 1650 TO THE PRESENT:
FROM TOWNLAND TO TERRACE GARDEN AND BEYOND

Brian P. Murphy, OSB

PAPAVER EDITIONS
LIMERICK

GLENSTAL ABBEY GARDENS: *c.* 1650 TO THE PRESENT

First published 2014

by Papaver Editions
'Mount Carmel'
4 Ballinacurra Terrace
Limerick
papavereditions@gmail.com

Credits for the photographs, when known, are given either beside the image or in the acknowledgements. Every effort has been made to trace the copyright holder of the illustrations included in this book and to ensure the accuracy of their captions.

Text copyright © 2014 Brian P. Murphy, OSB

The author has asserted his moral rights.

ISBN   978-0-9928220-0-2 (paperback)
        978-0-9928220-1-9 (hardback)

All rights reserved. The material in this publication is protected by copyright law. Except as may be permitted by law, no part of the material may be reproduced (including by storage in a retrieval system) or transmitted in any form or by any means; adapted; rented or lent without the written permission of the copyright owners.

British Library Cataloguing in Publication Data. A CIP catalogue record for this book is available from the British Library.

Printed and Design by Cube, Limerick.
10 9 8 7 6 5 4 3 2 1

DUM SPIRO SPERO
('WHILE I BREATHE, I HOPE')

To the 'men of the roads' whose help in restoring the Glenstal Gardens was invaluable

CONTENTS

Foreword *by Angela Coffey*	xiv - xix
Acknowledgements	xx - xxiii
Introduction	xxiv - 11
The Carbery Heritage	12 - 21
The Ilchester Oak	22 - 25
The Barrington Heritage	26 - 49
The End of the Barrington Era	50 - 57
The Benedictine Heritage	58 - 65
The Work of An Taisce	66 - 71
The First Stage of Restoration, 1986 – 2004	72 - 83
The Bible Garden: Idea and Design	84 - 101
Reflections on Bible Themes	102 - 111
The Second Stage of Restoration, 2005 to the Present	112 - 121
The Restoration of the Lady Garden	122 - 135
The Planting of the Ogham Tree Calendar	136 - 139

Foreword

I welcome this publication as a valuable record of our social history. More than 60 years ago, I became aware of Glenstal. My father, an early disciple of Muintir na Tíre, founded by Canon John Hayes (born near Glenstal), had been introduced by him to Fr Winoc, OSB, one the Belgian monks to arrive in Glenstal in 1927. Since 1950, I have attended the Christmas midnight. Mass at the abbey almost without a break. I distinctly remember when I was based in the United Nations Economic Commission for Western Asia in Beirut choosing to come home rather than go to Jerusalem for Christmas. Christmas Eve at Glenstal is so very special. It so happened that, subsequently, I 'settled down' to live in Newport within a 10 minute drive of the abbey and its school.

In the mid-1970s, when a degree of prosperity began to be established in Ireland and the major cities were designated as growth areas for inward investment, I became a committee member of the Limerick branch of An Taisce. I remarked at one meeting that the landscape at Glenstal was of local heritage significance and that the identification of the tree and shrub species there might be of great educational interest to many. Aesthetically, Glenstal is a glorious demesne *c.* 30 minutes from Limerick City. The mile-long avenue, a paradise for walkers, which leads up to the castle is flanked from mid-December onwards with the red and purple of the rhododendrons, the yellow blossoms of the azaleas and, my favourite, the fiery orange of the Chilean fire flame (*embothrium*); and that is only the beginning. To the west of the castle and the church is the Lady Garden, the fine limestone bridge leading to the Lady Garden, and in the glen are the remains of the ancient Mulryan Castle.

The beauty and variety of the Glenstal landscape is a tribute to the enlightenment of Sir Matthew and Lady Charlotte Barrington and to their family successors. Fr Brian has assembled the statistics of their tree planting and I could not resist the temptation to summarise how many trees had been planted: 143,350 in 1822/3; 126,400 in 1824; and 35,000 in 1825/6. Bowing our heads to Chekhov, Fr Brian also revealed that in

1842 Sir Matthew proposed a 'cherry orchard' at Glenstal. In 1974, our Limerick branch of An Taisce took its first steps to restore the Glenstal Estate and to make it better known to the public. Before long, the National Botanic Gardens had sent down its taxonimist, Dr Brian Morley, to initiate the identification of plants, shrubs and trees. The Benedictine community was, as ever, welcoming. I remember Brian Morley saying to me: 'look, whatever about identifying the trees and shrubs you really should see what can be done to restore the Terrace Garden. It is one of the jewels of the Irish landscape'. So, with the encouragement of Abbot Augustine O'Sullivan, we set about getting advice and fund-raising. Aesthetically we were greatly helped by the architect and garden designer Patrick Bowe. Then Liscannor slabs and kerbing were obtained and Roadstone (now CRH) donated the pathway chippings. Joe Kemmy, the stonemason of the well known Limerick family, took on the job of resetting the coping stones and pointing the stone walls. Cheques arrived from those who recognised the historical significance of the Terrace Garden restoration.

Abbot Augustine had reminded me that the monastic community were fully committed to their everyday work and that, consequently, the finished garden should be 'labour light'. I can only conclude that a Higher Authority was listening in! Brian Murphy came to Glenstal in 1984 and, since 1986, has combined his historical work with the restoration and upkeep of the gardens: not only the Terrace Garden, in which he has planted a Bible Garden, but also the Lady Garden and the surrounds of this ancient site. We are greatly indebted to him and his band of helpers: fellow members of the community, guests and men of the roads. This book not only gives an account of the work undertaken but also provides a valuable historical record of the place that is now known as Glenstal Abbey. We are deeply indebted to the Benedictine community at Glenstal for the welcome that it extends to the public to enjoy this exceptional amenity.

Angela Coffey

The gate lodge at the front entrance to Glenstal Abbey. Sketch by Eric Duhan.

Acknowledgements

Many thanks are owed to many people for their help in bringing this book to fruition. Many thanks are also owed to many people for their help in restoring the gardens of Glenstal, since I began working in them in 1986. I thank Margaret McDonnell for suggesting that a book should be written some years ago and for encouraging the completion of the work. Thanks to Fr Fintan Lyons who not only worked with me in the early days of the garden project but also regularly advised me to write a garden book. Thanks to Ruth Healy for her skill and patience in the scanning of many photographs and images during the past year. The help of Greg Ashe was also invaluable in this regard. Thanks to T.J. Ryan of Cube Printing Ltd for his professionalism and efficiency and Frederike Leclerc for her attention to detail and for her talent as a design artist. Thanks to Angus Mitchell for taking time out from his research and writing on Roger Casement and for making time to help with the final stages of bringing an unwieldy text to a publication.

I thank Jane Powers for allowing me to reproduce her article on the Bible Garden, which appeared in *The Irish Garden* (September/October 1996), and for the photographs, which were taken by her husband Jonathan Hession. Thanks to Eric Duhan for allowing me to use sketches, which formed part of his personal guide to the garden. Thanks to Finola Reid for allowing me to use photographs of the Lady Garden, which she took as part of her survey of the estate in 2003. Thanks to John Liddy for allowing me to use two of his poems that were written after his visits to the gardens in recent years. Acknowledgements to the Ordnance Survey Ireland for the use of their maps and to Trinity College Dublin, for the use of the Down Survey map. I thank many people for the use of their photographs: Fr Philip Tierney, Br Denis Hooper, Br Timothy McGrath, Fr Cyril Schaffer, Brian Mehigan, Irene Fenton and many others.

In regard to helpers in the garden, I have named them in the narrative of the text and to list them all now would lead to repetition. These helpers include: fellow members of the community, boys in the school, guests and other voluntary helpers. One particular group, the 'men of the roads', merits special attention. Their name in French, '*les hommes de voyage*', conjures up a more glamorous image of them – men on a journey, men seeking a way in life. Some were living rough; some were in hostels; some lived in social housing. Living in our hostel, which accommodated four men, they were cared for by Fathers Francis and John and many worked with myself in the garden. Their efforts in clearing the many abandoned areas of the estate were invaluable over many years. Sadly, a decision by the Health and Safety Executive that our hostel was not compatible with a school on the same site resulted in its closure some three years ago. In the narrative, I have devoted a special section to their efforts in restoring the gardens. In that section I explain the context in which Donegal Jim said to a visiting guest: '*dum spiro spero*' (while I breathe, I hope). Words that may be taken as a fitting motto for any gardener or, indeed, for anyone seeking a way through life, and explain why they have been taken as the motto of this book.

Brian P. Murphy, OSB

Introduction

The round tower of Glenstal Castle with the stone man, 'Pierre', standing near the flag pole.

The knight who stands on duty at the top of the turreted tower of Glenstal Castle is not all that he appears to be. He is carved of stone and proudly surveys the surrounding countryside. He was known to the Barrington family as Pierre, a pun on the French word for stone. The inscription that surrounds the top of the tower is also intended to deceive. It reads: 'Bardwell me fecit 1139' — 'Bardwell made me 1139', referring to the architect, William Bardwell. On closer inspection, it is possible to discern the real date, 1839. It was at this date that the first impressions of the large Norman style edifice began to make their mark on the landscape. Many more years, and many modifications of the plans, were to take place before work on the castle ended. Even then the original design was never brought to completion. However, the parkland demesne of some 400 acres, which surrounds the castle, was completed in the style that Matthew Barrington had selected from the very first days of the project. It is this parkland demesne that is the subject of this study. The story centres around the Barrington family; their acquisition of land in County Limerick; their building of a castle home in the nineteenth century; the earlier buildings and garden on part of their estate which date from the seventeenth century and earlier; and the developments on the property, after the Barrington family left in 1925 and were succeeded two years' later by a religious community of Benedictine monks.

Matthew Barrington (1788 –1861) was the inspiration behind the building of Glenstal Castle. The Barrington family could trace its lineage back to Norman times and its coming to Ireland to the campaigns of Cromwell. The tombstone of a Francis Barrington (d. 1683) in St Mary's Cathedral, would appear to mark their origins in Limerick City. A memorial tablet in the cathedral to Samuel Barrington, a maker of clocks, in 1693 provides a direct line of descent to Matthew Barrington. Although some of the family had been appointed sheriffs of Limerick in subsequent years, the family business was very much based on trade: firstly, that of clock making and, secondly, a pewter business. The first shop was on Broad Street; the second on Charlotte's Quay.

The Barrington family portrait, *c.* 1829, by Martin Cregan. Left to right: Daniel, son of Sir Joseph; Sir Matthew (1788–1861) eldest son of Sir Joseph; Sir William (1815–1872) eldest son of Sir Matthew; Sir Joseph (1764–1846); Sir Croker (1817–1890) second son of Sir Matthew; Samuel and Croker both sons of Sir Joseph. The scroll in the hands of Sir Matthew reads: 'ground plan of the hospital'. The dates are given of those who succeeded to the title.

The marriage of Matthew's father, Joseph (1764–1846), to Mary Baggott, the daughter of Daniel Baggott, the owner of a boot shop on Mary Street, did nothing to improve the social standing of the Barrington family. Most authorities also mention that Mary Baggott was a Catholic. Researching the matter further, and assisted by invaluable help from Pat Brosnan, a regular visitor to the abbey, it was found that the wedding of Joseph Barrington to Mary Baggott took place at St Mary's Roman Catholic Church, Athlunkard Street Limerick, on 7 August 1787. More remarkably the baptismal records of the same church revealed that Matthew Barrington was baptised there on 27 May 1788. The baptism was conducted by Fr William Goonan and the godparents were Daniel and Catherine Baggott. At this time Roman Catholics were barred from full participation in civic life (the Act of Roman Catholic Emancipation ameliorating their condition was only passed in 1829) and such a marriage and, indeed, baptism appeared certain to limit the social and civic ambitions of the Barrington family.

Despite these origins, the family improved their personal wealth and their standing in the civic life of Limerick. Matthew, himself, was well educated and he qualified as a lawyer with offices on both George's Street, Limerick, and 13 FitzWilliam Strect, Dublin. Details of his life at this time are hard to obtain and much more research is required. However, it seems reasonable to presume that, in order to advance his career, he must, at some time, have changed his religious denomination. Two events in 1814, enabled him to advance his position in life: firstly, on 1 January 1814, he married Charlotte Hartigan and he received not only a dowry of some £2,000 but also some land in County Limerick; and, secondly, he was appointed crown solicitor for Munster with a salary of £15,000 per annum. This financial security enabled Matthew Barrington to take the first steps towards the building of his castle home. On 11 December 1818, he leased, from the descendants of the late Lord Carbery (the family name was Evans), the townlands of Cappercullen, Garranbane, Meentulla and Glenstal in East Limerick some 10 miles from

Limerick City. The annual rent was £150. Original research by two deceased members of the Glenstal community, Fr Hubert Janssens and Fr Mark Tierney, provides invaluable information about the Barrington family. Their articles in the *Old Limerick Journal* (winter 1988) on 'The Barringtons of Limerick' and 'Sir Matthew Barrington: 1788–1861,' and Fr Mark's book, *Murroe and Boher* (1966) provides more detail not only on the Barrington family but also on their predecessors in the Murroe area.

In the same year, 1818, Barrington moved from the family home on Barrington Street, Limerick City, to Clonkeen some five miles from the city. He also had a house at 50 St Stephen's Green, Dubin as well as his legal offices. To facilitate his access to Clonkeen, Matthew Barrington constructed a wrought-iron bridge over the Killeengarrif River, a tributary of the Mulcair River, which flows at the bottom of the house's garden. The bridge still stands with the inscription 'Erected in 1818 by M. Barrington'. The name Barrington's Bridge soon became a recognised place name and appeared as such on maps of the area. The house became known as Barrington's' Bridge House. From this location it was possible for Matthew Barrington to supervise the improvements planned for his recently leased land.

Before work began on the newly acquired property, Charlotte Barrington made a copy of the county map of the area. She completed her work in 1819. The map depicted the Barony of Owneybeg, which was part of Clanwilliam in County Limerick. An extraordinary work of art measuring three feet by two feet, it presented a coloured representation of the area that Matthew planned to develop. Townlands were designated in a fine script; houses of the gentry were carefully drawn and ancient church sites were clearly indicated. It provided an ideal base upon which Matthew Barrington could plan and execute his grand design. The names of the townlands that Barrington had leased were described in their more ancient names: for example, Glanstahill, Meengnatulla and Garranbaun. Cappercullen was represented in its modern spelling as was Moher. The main property of the Carbery family, Cappercullen House and garden, featured prominently on the map and was to become a prominent feature of the Barrington parkland estate.

A townland was a small geographical division of land, which was used in Ireland and which was of Gaelic origin. There are some 60,000 townlands in the parishes of Ireland. Owing to the manner in which the Barrington family named their family home as Glenstal Castle, a certain element of mystery surrounds its location. Although called Glenstal, it is actually located in the townland of Garranbane. Apparently, and this is part of the family folklore, Matthew Barrington did not like the name of Garranbane for his castle and selected, instead, the name of the neighbouring townland of Glenstal, which he also owned. Even today, however, the postal authorities observe the ancient usage of the townland names for official post: for example, voting forms for general elections are still addressed to members of the Benedictine community as residents of Garranbane, Murroe, County Limerick. There are some 40 townlands in the parish of Murroe and they comprise c. 17,500 acres: Cappercullen has 322 acres, Garranbane 1,033 acres and Glenstal 1,013 acres.

Not on the map, but worthy of mention in terms of the historic origins of the land, is the hill of Liosavurra, in Irish, Lios Ghuaire. This high hill, about a mile from the castle site, is situated on the back road to Newport. As described by my confrere Fr Seán Ó Duinne, 'it is a large Hill Fort with a Lios or Rath encircling the summit of the hill and appears to have been one of the outposts of the King of Cashel'. Previous to this it was a megalithic site with a tomb and stone pillars, which have been removed. It was also the site of two annual fairs at Bealtaine and Samhain. In mythological terms, the hill is a supernatural dwelling of the Tuatha Dé Danann. It is sacred to the local goddess Eibhliu daughter of Guaire and it is from her that the surrounding mountain gets its name, Slivefelim, in Irish, Sliabh Eibhlinne. While not showing Liosavurra,

Charlotte Barrington's map of East County Limerick, 1819, showing most of the 9,500 acres which the Barrington family acquired and also the site of the ancient Cistercian Abbey at Abington. The map was reproduced with the help of Patricia Macnamara.

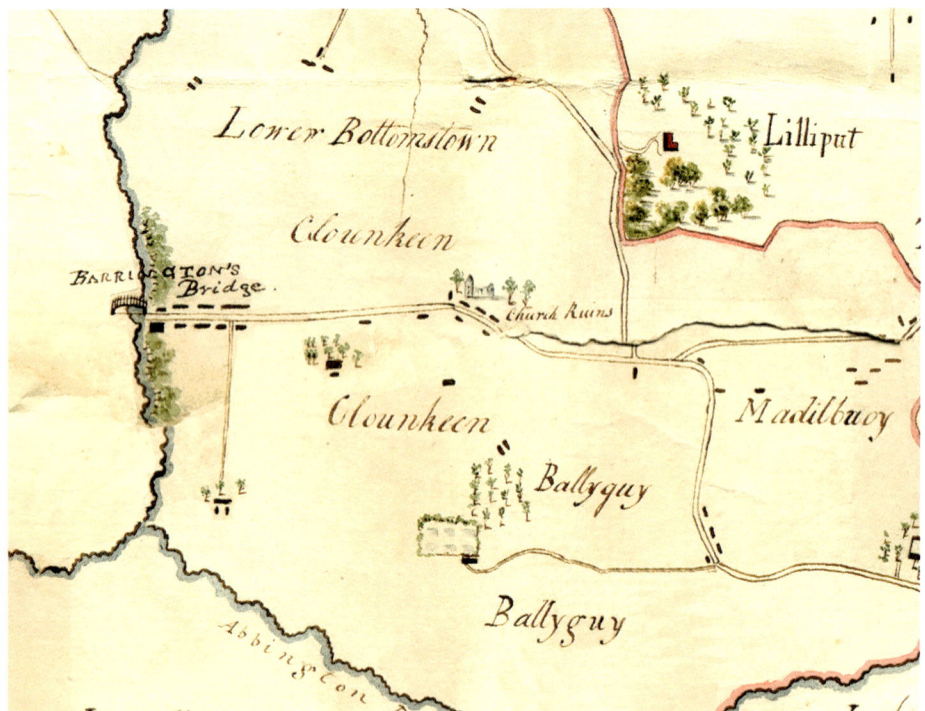

Detail of the 1819 map showing Barrington's Bridge and the ruins of Clonkeen Church.

Charlotte Barrington's map did depict the trees, lakes, glens and local houses to striking effect. A range of mountains was shown above Cappercullen House extending to the townland of Glanstahill. Houses were also depicted: for example, Ashrow (*sic*) belonging to the Evans (Carbery) family; Glebe House of the Church of Ireland minister of Abington; and Castle Comfort, the newly built house of the Roman Catholic priest of Murroe. Barrington's Bridge was also indicated on the map. The bridge, with almost symbolic significance, marked the entry point into the Barony of Owneybeg. It was from that point that Matthew Barrington, having surveyed the landscape drawn by his wife, advanced inland to implement the plans for his dream castle and estate.

Detail of the 1819 map showing Cappercullen Estate, Murroe and the Old Factory.

Glenstal Abbey Gardens 11

The Carbery Heritage

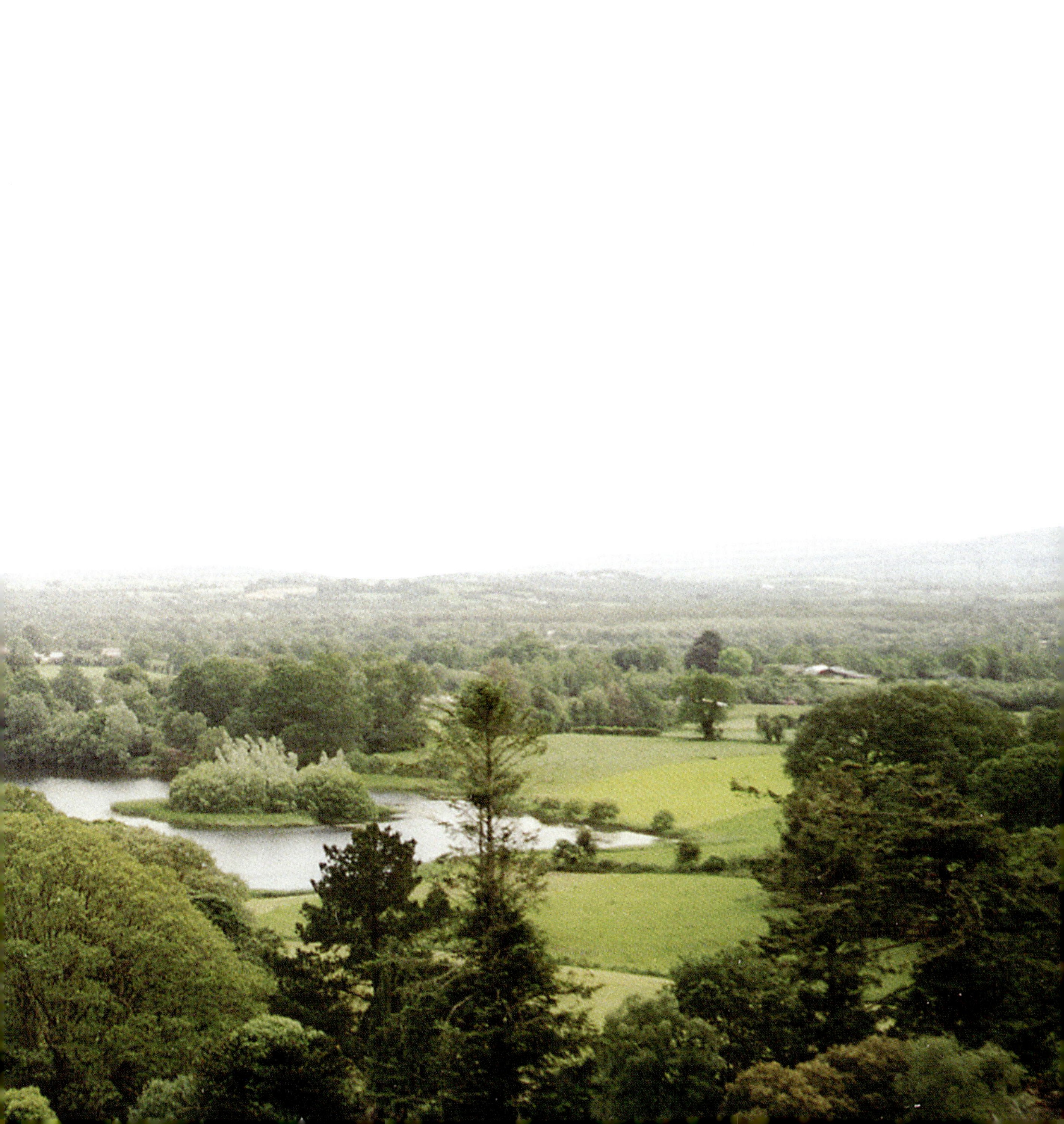

The most striking part of the Carbery Estate that Barrington had leased was the walled terraced garden. It dates from *c.* 1680 and still remains intact as do other ruins of a more ancient past. For that reason, some consideration of the Carbery heritage is fitting. John Evans, of Welsh extraction, came to Limerick in the reign of King James 1 (1603–25) and his son and grandson, both named George, were responsible for the acquisition and development of the Cappercullen property. George Evans, his eldest son, served in the army that suppressed the rebellion of 1641 and, in return for his loyalty to King Charles 1 (1642–49), he received land at Ballygrennan, County Limerick, and other land in County Cork. It is this George Evans who was responsible for the acquisition of the land in Cappercullen and the surrounding area in the following years: firstly, by leasing the land and, secondly, by buying it outright. His name appears several times as part of the Cromwellian settlement of County Limerick, which was based on the Down Survey. This detailed and mapped survey of land ownership in Ireland was compiled under the direction of William Petty between the years 1655–58. It built upon the work of an earlier civil survey and was designed to form the basis for land settlement in Ireland following the successful reoccupation of Ireland by Oliver Cromwell (1649–58). George Evans is listed as owning 127 acres in the townland of Cappercullen (spelt Capaghcullin), 95 acres in the townland of Morrow, other land in Muroewood and 98 acres in Boarmanshill. All of these townlands were in the parish of Abbeyowney. The Down survey also shows a house with turrets on the Cappercullen site. Abstracts from the Calendar of Cappercullen Papers detail the manner in which George Evans added to his original land acquisitions in the area: on 1 March 1665 he received, from John Taylor, some 605 acres in the area of Cappercullen and Puckane for the sum of £45; on 26 February 1680, he received, from Patrick Walsh, the remainder of his land in Cappercullen (*c.* 139 acres) for the sum of £1,000. All of these transactions are recorded in the Calendar of Cappercullen Papers that are to be found in an appendix to Fr Mark Tierney's book

Ruins of Cappercullen House, *c.* 1600, which was built on the site of the Mulryan Castle. This house was associated with one of Sheridan Le Fanu's ghost stories. Watercolour sketch by Mona Lawless, 2013.

Glenstal Abbey Gardens

Detail from the Down Survey map (*c.* 1655) of the Parish of Abbeyowney showing Cappercullen (Capacullyn) with an image of Mulryan Castle and house.

timber wood (7)

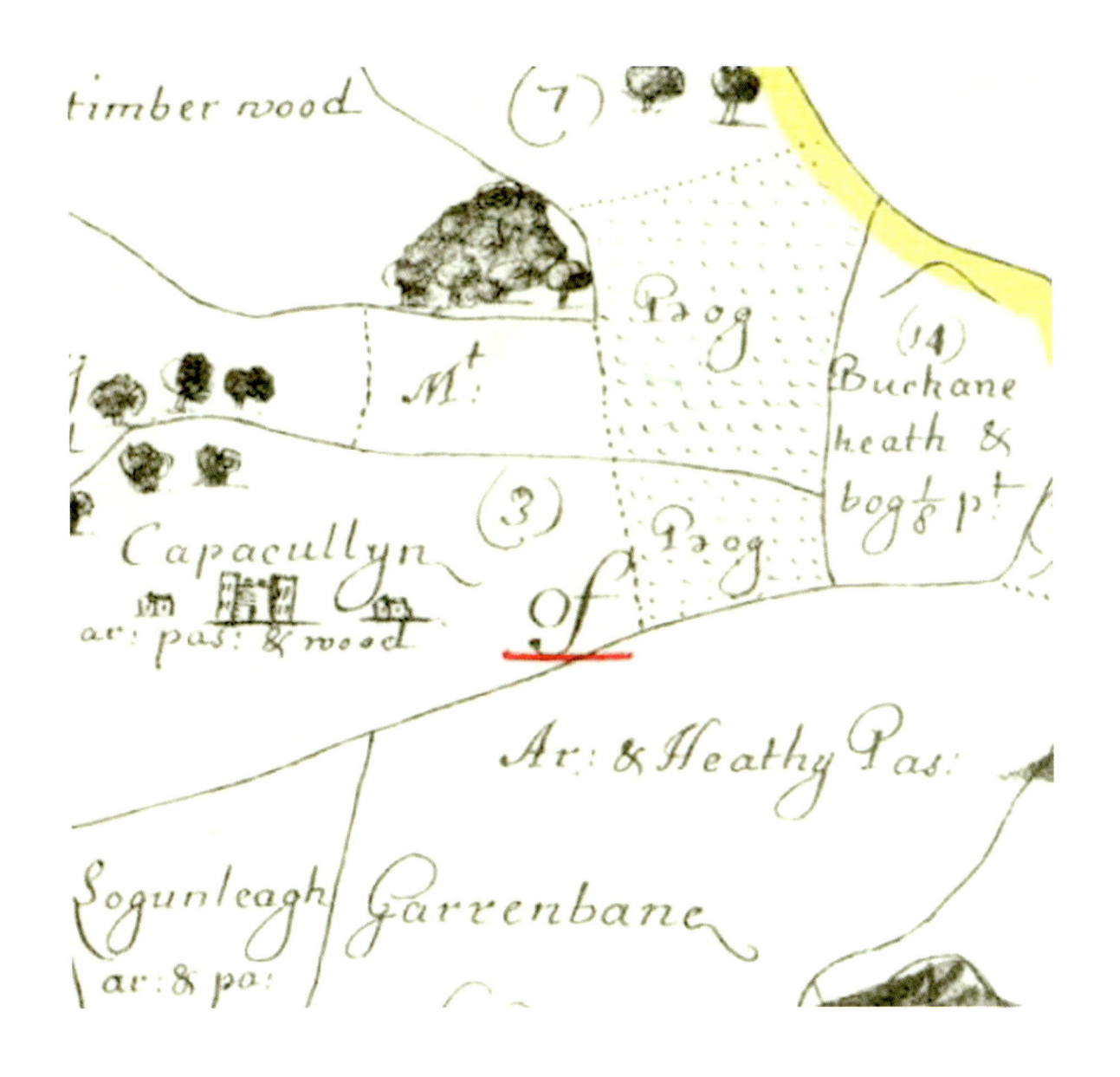

Bog

M.t

(14) Buckane heath & bog ⅛ p.t

(3) Capacullyn Bog
ar: pas: & wood of

Ar: & Heathy Pas:

Sogunleagh Garrenbane
ar: & pa:

Glenstal Abbey Gardens 17

on *Murroe and Boher*. James Grene Barry in his *Cromwellian Settelement of the County of Limerick* has provided an excellent summary of these land arrangements and the recent Trinity College computerised presentation of the Down Survey is invaluable. The transaction with John Taylor of 1665 refers to the Castle of Cappercullen and a document of 1699 refers to a bill for the glass work detail from the work performed on Cappercullen House and stables. Although the name of Joseph Stepney, a landowner at Abington, has been associated with the building of the Terrace Garden, the documents do not suggest that he held the land in Cappercullen at that time. A letter from one of the Le Fanu family to Fr Hubert, in which it was claimed that Stepney built the garden, would appear to be the origin of the story.

Traces of the foundations of Cappercullen Castle may still be seen on the top of the western side of the glen and the gable end of a house rises above the glen inside the contours of the old castle. In the glen, itself, there is a Mass Rock which marks the place where Mass was said during the eighteenth century, when public celebration of the Roman Catholic Mass was prohibited by law. The castle is associated with the Mulryan family who moved into the area *c.* 1400. Fr Hubert Janssens, in an unpublished article, stated that 'at the time of the Anglo–Norman invasion the proprietors of this district were the O'Heffernans and the O'Callans, names which are not to be found anymore in the barony. The O'Mulryans, a Leinster sept from the Kilkenny–Carlow border, dispossessed them, probably as late as the fifteenth century'. From their base in Cappercullen, the Mulryans became the most influential family in the parish of Abbeyowney. The extent of their power was illustrated by a petition from the abbot of Abington to Sir James Butler, earl of Ormond, on 31 May 1436. The petition is to be found in Mark Tierney's book *Murroe and Boher*. The abbot reminded the duke that

> no one was to be received or admitted as a monk therein, especially to the dignity of the aforesaid abbacy, unless he

were a man of English race: nevertheless, a certain Dermot O'Gleeson, a professed monk from some other place, sprung from the Irish nation, against the royal statutes and mandates, by the inordinate power of laymen and especially of the chief men of the Irish, viz. Cornelius O'Mulrian, pretends that he is de facto abbot of the said monastery.

The petition makes clear not only the emerging power of the Mulryan family but also the racial undertones underlying the foundation of the abbey. Ten months after the petition, the Pope appointed an English abbot of the monastery. However, by the mid-sixteenth century, members of the Mulryan clan were abbots of Abington Abbey and John Mulrian was the abbot at the time of its closure in the reign of Henry VIII. It is fascinating to recall that the land of this abbey, situated some five miles from Cappercullen, and founded in 1206 during the reign of King John (1199–1216), is now, some 800 years later, once again in the care of monks.

Following the Reformation, the Mulryan family lost its influence at Abington and following the Elizabethan land settlement, it lost its possessions at Cappercullen. Indeed, the name of O'Mulryan, identified as 'a Catholic', is recorded as the previous owner of the nearby land at Boarmanshill prior to its acquisition by George Evans. Here, in summary outline, consists the historic importance of the Barrington gardens: not only is one able to trace the creation of a fine parkland estate in the nineteenth century, but one is also able to identify the transforming forces that led to changes in land ownership and land cultivation in Ireland from the sixteenth century. The first major transformation was the building of a walled terraced garden to the west of the ruins of Cappercullen Castle and Cappercullen House by George Evans in *c.* 1680.

The garden, as with many gardens of this period, may well have been constructed with a defensive purpose in mind. Outside the walled garden, and running for about one mile in the direction of Murroe, are the walls enclosing a deer park. A charter of King Charles II of England and Ireland, dated 31 July 1682, and ratified by the High Court of Chancery in Dublin, on 20 June 1683, provide precise dates for this park. The charter, conferred at the king's court at Windsor, granted permission to George Evans, 'the younger', to establish a deer park on his land at Cappercullen and Murroe in the Barony of Owneybeg. The grant also conferred upon Evans the same hunting rights for a deer park at another of his properties, Caherass, near Croom, County Limerick.

The naming of George Evans (1655–1720), the younger, as the owner of the deer park indicates clearly that, by that time, he was responsible for the estate at Cappercullen. Similarly the dates on the charter, and the delineation of the deer park, confirm that the walled garden was in existence *c.* 1680. The area of the park was to be *c.* 500 acres and not only permitted the hunting of deer but also allowed for the creation of warrens for other animals. A raised and fortified walkway, running from

◂ Some of the remains of the Mulryan Castle, *c.* 1400, near the bridge on the western side of Cappercullen Glen

a corner of the walled garden, served to protect Cappecullen House and garden from the deer and enabled one to survey the deer park and the hills beyond. All of these features are marked on the map of the 'Record of Monuments and Places' that has been issued by the Office of Public Works.

As with the garden, this walkway also served a defensive purpose. It should be recalled that the war between James II (1685–88) and William III (1689–1702) took place in Ireland between the years 1688–91. James had been forced to abdicate at the end of 1688 and William had been selected by the English Parliament, in January 1689, as his successor in order to preserve 'the welfare of this Protestant kingdom'. The war, therefore, had a distinctly religious, as well as an ethnic character. It only ended with the Treaty of Limerick in October 1691 and a victory for the cause of William III. During the war, George Evans, as a supporter of William III, may well have needed protection from the native Irish who supported James II and Patrick Sarsfield, his leading general in the Limerick area. According to Debrett's *Peerage & Baronetage*, George Evans became a privy councillor after the war and was returned as an MP for Charleville in County Cork. He declined a peerage in the reign of George I. He had married Mary Eyre of Galway in 1679 and his main residence was Bulgaddon Hall, Kilmallock, County Limerick. His son, George Evans (1680–1749), who also made his home at Bulgaddon Hall, accepted a peerage from George I in 1715 as Lord Carbery. From that date the name of Carbery was associated with the Cappercullen property. Although not resident at Cappercullen, Lord Carbery made plans, in 1717, to build a new house of brick on a site to the south of the walled garden. He also built a hunting lodge near the Factory House at Cappanhana, which is a townland adjoining Cappercullen. Recently, in October 2012 a painting was sold at Christies auction house in London of George Evans, the first Lord Carbery, 'stag hunting with his hounds'. It is a fine painting of the Irish School, *c.* 1740.

The Ilchester Oak

The Ilchester Oak in 1809. Sketch by Lady Louisa Lansdowne (1785–1851), the daughter of Mary Theresa O'Grady, who often met her future husband under this tree.

Mary Theresa O'Grady (c. 1755–1790), second countess of Ilchester, with her daughter Elizabeth. Portrait by Thomas Beech (1777).

Lord Henry Thomas (1747–1802) who married Mary Theresa O'Grady in 1772 and who became the second earl of Ilchester in 1776.

In August 1759, the new Cappercullen House, the deer park and 'the fairs of Murroe' were leased to Standish O'Grady of Elton, County Limerick for a yearly rent of £225. This transaction took place when a third Lord Carbery held the title. The O'Grady family (sometimes called Grady) left one distinctive, if fragile, mark upon the parkland estate: the oak tree on the left of the front avenue as one enters the property. It is under the shade of this tree that Mary O'Grady (1755–90), the daughter of the house, is said to have courted an English soldier before marrying him in 1772. The marriage of Mary O'Grady to a soldier is a historical reality: the soldier's father visited the O'Grady family before giving his consent to the marriage and, having seen the young woman, he granted his approval. This man, much to the surprise of the O'Grady family, turned out to be the earl of Ilchester and his soldier son was Lord Henry Thomas Stavordale. For that reason, the tree has always been known as the Ilchester oak and was known as such by the Barrington family. The outline of the story is given in Fr Mark's book *Murroe and Boher* and his subsequent contacts

Glenstal Abbey Gardens

with the Ilchester family provided further confirmation of the story. Remarkably, two finely drawn contemporary sketches of the tree and of the O'Grady house were found to exist. More remarkably, the two sketches, both drawn on 27 September 1809, were drawn by Lady Louisa Lansdowne, the daughter of Mary O'Grady. Louisa Emma was born in 1785 and married Henry Petty-Fitzmaurice, third marquess of Lansdowne in 1808. The Fitzmaurice family were earls of Kerry and this association may have occasioned the visit of Lady Louisa Lansdowne to Ireland in 1809, the year after her marriage and the year that she created the sketches. It is of interest that someone living in a townland depicted on the Down Survey should marry into the family of Lord Lansdowne, the title given to William Petty for his work in compiling the Down Survey. The house that was sketched by Louisa Lansdowne in 1809 was in a ruined condition: the O'Grady family no longer lived in it and the direct lineage of the Carbery's ended in March 1807 with

The 1809 sketch of Cappercullen House as redrawn from an earlier sketch by Lady Louisa Lansdowne. The House was situated directly to the south of the Terrace Garden.

CAPPERCULLEN HOUSE circa 1800

the death of John Evans, the fifth Lord Carbery. His daughter, Frances Dorothea, had married William Preston in 1789, and it was the heirs of that family with whom Matthew Barrington conducted most of the land transactions in acquiring the property. Eventually, the Carbery lineage was renewed with the Evans Freke family in County Cork and survives to this day.

The fragile condition of the Ilchester Oak today. Despite the damage caused by the great storm of 12th February 2014, when over 200 trees on the Glenstal estate were destroyed, this oak tree survived.

1829
Oct. & Nov. —

600 Rhododen[dron]
200 Guelder
2,000 Bird Ch[erry]
5,000 hazel
5,000 Do — Y[?]
1,000 Hunting[don?]
1,000 Red [Ho?]

The Barrington Heritage

nas	Ja edges
Roses	Woods
ny	
3 yr. old c	Thuring of
ung	Liverpool
Willow	
ew D	

Matthew Barrington was well aware of these ancient remains of the Carbery heritage but, in the early 1820s, as he had not yet purchased the property outright from the heirs of the Evans family, it made sense to make improvements on other fronts before proceeding to make plans for a house. A large notebook, entitled 'Memorandum as to Planting,' (1822–50) records the number of trees that were planted. It recounts that 'in the month of September, 1822, I agreed with Mr Arthur Baylor of Fermoy, to plant part of the Land of Glenstal in the county of Limerick'. The trees were to consist of oak, ash, elm, beech, sycamore and birch to be planted eight feet apart; and scotch fir, larch and spruce to be planted four feet apart. The trees were to be planted 'to the satisfaction of M. Barrington in a proper manner'; and it noted that 'the fences are made at the expense of Mr Barrington'. These references indicate that the memorandum was compiled by someone who was carrying out the tree planting at the direction of Matthew Barrington. The record continues that in 'the years 1823, 1824 and 1825 I made similar agreements with him for planting trees of said estate'. In the first plantation, from October 1822 to spring 1823, 66,000 hardwood trees were planted and 77,000 trees in a nursery. In the second plantation, in the following year, c. 50,000 hardwood trees were planted, among them were 20,000 ash, 13,000 oak, 30,000 Scotch fir and 8,000 sycamore.

A third plantation was undertaken from October 1824 to spring 1825 in the hills near Belvidere, an area in the north of the townland of Garranbane. In that year, the scale of tree planting was equally impressive: 14,500 oak, 10,800 ash, 6,700 beech, 2,800 birch, 3,000 sycamore and 1,600 mountain ash. A further 44,000 trees were planted in nurseries, among them larch (12,500) and Scotch fir (20,600). 4,000 whitethorn and 3,000 holly trees were also planted in hedges and underwood. The following year, 1825/6, the tree planting continued on the same level and 35,000 trees were planted for timber. These trees were planted in the glen near the bridge, which divided the townlands of Garranbane and Cappercullen. At

Detail from the Memorandum of Planting, 1823.

2

Barrington — and the Underwood in the plantations and the Quicks &c in the hedges have been provided by him —

	Charlotte Rock – back of Davoren's house & front of it 1st plantation, to River	hard Wood for Standards	Nurses	Underwood & hedges
From Oct. 1822 to Spring 1823				
Oaks		18,500		
Ash		21,800		
Elm		200		
Beech		14,000		
Birch		8,800		
Sycamore		2,350		
M. Ash		500		
Larch			20,000	
Scotch Fir			36,000	
Silver D⁰			200	
Spruce D⁰			10,000	
Alder			11,000	
		66,150	77,200	
also Wild Cherry Trees				
Total — 143,350				

N.1 — In Nov. 1825 Hazel Nuts & Acorns sown &c through plantation for Underwood

the same time, the planting of trees in nurseries increased from *c.* 44,000 to 79,200. Mr Ryan of Belvidere, who became known as Ryan Belvidere, was responsible for one of these nurseries.

In 1828, it was recorded that a nursery was laid out 'by the advise of Mr McLeish who prepared the mountain at Davern's house'. While that work was being carried out, some seedlings were preserved in a nursery at Lord Limerick's garden, which were later transferred to this Glenstal plot. The planting of timber continued on a grand scale in 1829: in early February, over 130,000 trees were bought from O'Keeffe's of Dublin — 20,000 oak, 30,000 ash, 20,000 birch and 60,000 alder; and later in the month more trees were bought from Simpson's of Dublin — *c.* 2,000 Bedford willow and *c.* 2,000 Canada poplar. In March, *c.* 235,000 trees were bought from O'Keeffe's of Dublin — 130,000 larch, 100,000 Scotch fir, 3,000 Silver fir and 5,000 Spruce fir; and, at the end of the month, 50 rhododendrons were bought from Dooly's of Nenagh.

The acquisition of rhododendrons was the first step in the buying of ornamental trees. In the last months of 1829, 600 rhododendrons were bought from Thrings of Liverpool and, along with many other trees, were designated to be planted along the edges of the woods. Apart from the rhododendrons, there were 200 guelder roses, 2,000 bird cherry, 200 dogwood, 25 tulip trees and many more specimens. Early in 1830, 70 arbutus trees and 150 Portuguese laurel were sourced from Killarney and, as the year ended, Baylor of Fermoy sent 200 laurel and 4,000 apple trees. The year ended with the receipt from Liverpool of 2,000 Spanish chestnuts, 3,000 hazel, 2,000 weeping birch, 1,000 Ontario poplar and 1,000 cherry trees.

Remarkably, Matthew Barrington engaged in this enormous operation of tree planting while he was also fully occupied not only with his own legal work but also in the building of a hospital for the poor in Limerick City. Work on the building started in 1829 and, by an act of parliament in the following year, the 60-bed hospital was officially opened. It was designed by Frederick Darley and

Title page of the book *Essays on Landscape Gardening* (1825) by Richard Morris and signed by Matthew Barrington, London, July 1934. This book played a major part in the design of the Glenstal Castle parkland estate.

ESSAYS
ON
LANDSCAPE GARDENING,
AND ON UNITING
PICTURESQUE EFFECT
WITH
RURAL SCENERY:

CONTAINING

DIRECTIONS FOR LAYING OUT AND IMPROVING THE GROUNDS

CONNECTED WITH A

COUNTRY RESIDENCE.

ILLUSTRATED BY SIX PLATES.

BY RICHARD MORRIS, F.L.S.

SECRETARY TO THE MEDICO-BOTANICAL SOCIETY OF LONDON, AND AUTHOR OF
"THE BOTANIST'S MANUAL."

LONDON:
PRINTED FOR J. TAYLOR, AT THE ARCHITECTURAL LIBRARY,
HIGH HOLBORN.
1825.

Image from the book by Richard Morris entitled *Essays on Landscape Gardening, and on Uniting Picturesque Effect with Rural Scenery* showing three possible sites for a great house. Sir Mathew Barrington chose the middle position for Glenstal.

it was built on land that Matthew Barrington had acquired on the side of George's Quay, which fronted the Abbey River. It had cost £10,000 and immediately became an important feature of life in Limerick. Matthew's father, Joseph (1764–1846), was created a baronet in 1831, largely in recognition for the building of the hospital. Having completed the hospital and having secured a baronetcy for his family, Matthew Barrington immediately turned his attention to securing the lands that he had leased from the Carbery family in 1818. Late in 1831, he finalised his holding, 'when he paid the princely sum of £30,193..15s..10d for the Carbery estate'. Other transactions were necessary in later years in order to clarify remaining issues with the Carbery family but Matthew Barrington was free, after 1831, to consult with architects about plans for his castle home.

Architects submitted plans to Matthew Barrington from 1833 to 1836: William O'Hara, 1833; James and George Pain, 1833; Decimus Burton, 1834 and William Bardwell, 1836. Finally, the design of Bardwell was selected and work began on the building in 1836. The first phase of the building lasted until 1839. During the process of discussion over the design plans that had been submitted, Barrington's vision for his castle and parkland estate became strongly influenced by a book that he had bought in London. The book was by Richard Morris and was entitled *Essays on Landscape Gardening, and on Uniting Picturesque Effect with Rural Scenery*: 'containing Directions for Laying out and Improving the Grounds connected with a Country Residence'. The book was published in 1825 and Matthew Barrington signed his copy, London, July 1834. The theme of the book suited Barrington's purposes admirably. Moreover, it contained six illustrations, three of which were coloured, to illustrate the ideals outlined on the title page. One can almost see him choosing the site for his castle as he made pencil annotations in the margin of the book. 'If a situation too elevated be chosen,' he noted, 'however important the building and extensive the prospects from it, or impressive

Image from the book by Richard Morris entitled *Essays on Landscape Gardening, and on Uniting Picturesque Effect with Rural Scenery* showing access to a great house by winding avenues; a suggestion that was adopted by Sir Matthew Barrington for Glenstal Castle.

the view from it, much of its grandeur will be lost from deficiency of a wooded back-ground: it will also be too much exposed to bleak and cutting winds.'

These considerations ruled out the townland of Glenstal: it was the highest part of the estate which he had purchased and he had already carried out an extensive planting of trees for timber on it. Subsequent ideas in the book by Morris directed Barrington's thoughts to the townland of Garranbane: 'the best site for showing a villa to advantage', he noted with his pencil, 'is on the brow or near the summit of a wooded hill of moderate elevation; it is also the best situation for the introduction of ornamental and decorative accessories, as well in the gardens and in the shrubberies, in accordance with the buildings or with a bold and extensive scenery'. The first coloured plate at the back of the book illustrated this principle to perfection: the two houses depicted on the high and low points of the terrain were shown to ill-effect, while the house drawn near the brow of a hill was shown with a sunny prospect and a pleasant wooded background behind it. Inspired by these reflections, Barrington rejected as a site for his castle not only the high point of the Glenstal townland but also the lower-lying townland of Cappercullen. He then proceeded with Bardwell, his architect, to build his castle in the townland of Garranbane.

Matthew Barrington would also appear to have been influenced by Morris's book in his selection of the type of entrance that would lead to his house. He rejected a long straight avenue and opted for a winding road on the principle, as Morris put it, that 'when the road is conducted in a winding direction, the object now hidden, now viewed to advantage, the imagination is excited by the variety'. Moreover, Barrington noted that 'an occasional view of the house through the trees has a good effect; and from some part of the road a burst of view, and as good a prospect of the mansion as possible, should be presented, that the first impression may be favourable'. The second of the coloured plates illustrated the value of this curved approach to the house: starting from a gate lodge at the entrance to the estate, the avenue winds through the park, lakes and lawns until it comes upon the house. An oval of avenue then surrounds the house and links up with the domestic offices, the stables, the kitchen garden, the orchard and the flower garden.

The concept was both imaginative and practical. Clearly influenced by these considerations, Barrington did not make use of the former entrance to Cappercullen House, which had been created by its first owner, George Evans, and which was carefully delineated on the map drawn by his wife in 1819. Instead, he created a mile-long avenue, which wended its way through the fields of the deer park that had been granted to George Evans by King Charles II in 1683 and, which, in turn, was set amidst the oak trees of an ancient forest. The end result of Matthew Barrington's application of the ideals set out in Morris's book may be seen to this day in both the approach to Glenstal Castle and in the walks that surround it. Indeed, they were visible on the Ordnance Survey map of 1840 thus showing that work on the construction of avenues and walks went hand in hand with the building of the castle. The walled garden, known as the Lady Garden and associated with Lady Charlotte Barrington, is depicted on the map; so also is the earlier walled terraced garden, which dates back to George Evans and the 1680s.

The evidence indicates that Matthew Barrington was responsible not only for the planning of the parkland estate but also for the planting that took place within it. A manuscript 'Memorandum on Planting and Farming, 1842', contains several pages devoted to a 'General Plan' for Glenstal. In regard to the terrace, running along the southern length of the house, Barrington noted that 'I have musk and morrietta roses and jasmine to run up the terrace walls, and honeysuckle and clematis (white, purple and blue)' at the top. On the lower level of the terrace, he indicated that 'the choicest flowers of the garden', such as gentians, verbena and lobelia should be planted in parterres. He planned a pinetum at the side of the

Sir Matthew Barrington's general plan for Glenstal with specific suggestions for the planting of the terrace in front of the castle.

Glenstal — General Plan —

The Terrace runs along the Southern length of the House, extending to the Western side also —

Have Musk & noisette Roses & Jasmine to run up the Terrace Walls, & Honeysuckles & Clematis (White Purple & Blue) to Cluster at Top —

Vases with Gourd's Green & Golden fruit & other plants may be on Terrace — While the heads of a Mass of Crimson Roses & Strawberry coloured Hollyhocks spring from the Bank below —

On the lower level should be collected the choicest flowers of the garden, Gentianella, Verbena Lobelia, in their Parterres, with Colours as brilliant as old Painted Windows —

A Walk round to the Kitchen Garden, splendid in Autumn with Hollyhocks, Dahlias, China Asters, Nasturtians & African Marigolds — to the Glen

The Drives & Walks outside the fenced Ground lose themselves in the Thorn Hazel & holly Thickets which bound & fill up the plantations within the Park —

The Walk from Terrace into the Glen &c is thro the Rock which forms the base of the Terrace itself — Rock plants of every description should be planted, & also a profusion of the best exquisite climbing castle and advised that 'the trees be planted distant from each other so that hereafter their branches may not touch'. The pinetum still remains. For Cappercullen Glen, he proposed a fernery and the construction of several waterfalls, including 'a sheet of water', or small lake, opposite the old house of Belvidere. Barrington also proposed that 'in some part of the ground' there should be a cherry orchard with a few good eating-apple trees; and, in the margin, he added that the 'old garden at Cappercullen' was the best site for this. A note in the margin stated that Charlotte Barrington, his wife, recommended Eve apples as best for tarts and the Kerry and Golden Pippins as good apples.

The thoughts and suggestions made by Barrington could only have been made by someone who had a love and knowledge of gardens and parkland estates. That Barrington had such a knowledge and love is confirmed by the many newpaper clippings from *The Gardeners' Chronicle* that are to be found in the 'Memorandum'. Dating from the early 1840s, they provide detailed information on such diverse matters as fruit trees, pine trees, the making of garden walks (that is the material structure of the walk), underwood planting, climbing plants, a rosetum and rhododendrons. Many of the articles were annotated with Barrington's well informed comments. While these developments in regard to the parkland estate were taking place, Barrington continued with his extensive programme of tree planting.

In November 1830, a huge selection of trees was sent from Liverpool: 2,000 Spanish chestnuts, 3,000 hazel, 2,000 weeping birch, 1,000 Ontario poplars, 1,000 cherry trees and 200 large Onatario poplars. In February 1832, it was recorded that many trees had been sent from Dublin and had been planted in two new nursery plantations by Arthur Baylor in the upper part of the mountains, presumably the high ground around Glenstal and Belvidere. Among the trees were 5,000 oak; 10,000 spruce; 40,000 larch and 10,000 Scotch fir. In November 1833, more trees were planted in the nursery at Belvidere. Apart from the large trees, such as 500 scarlet oak, there were 500 Portugal laurel, 100 rhododendrons, 100 scarlet dogwood and 100 China roses. In subsequent years, when planting was taking place in the parkland estate, varieties of laurel, rhododendrons, magnolia, syringa, roses and other shrubs were ordered regularly. For example, in 1839, from Hegarty's nursery in Wicklow, Barrington received 100 specimens of the following shrubs: snowberry, *arbutus*, *rhododendron*, *hydrangea*, Portugal laurel, *lauristinus* and *syringa*. The cost of each batch of 100 was £1.

Tree planting, on this enormous scale, continued even while work on the castle was suspended for a time at the end of the 1830s. For example, in 1844, Matthew Barrington received, from Hodgens of Limerick, 2,000 sweet briars, 300 assorted roses, 200 *Aucuba japonica*, 100 *Azalea pontica*, 100 Virginian dogwood, 100 rhododendron maximum hybrid, 25 scarlet rhododendrons, 20 large *Garrya elliptica* and other shrubs such as *magnolia*, sumach and *berberis*.

Barrington noted that 'a great number of *Leycesteria formosa*' (pheasant berry) had also been delivered and he instructed that 'they should be at once opened and planted out in the nursery'. The remains of this shrub still dominate parts of the estate. At the end of the year, 1844, Barrington showed that he was still prepared to plan on a grand scale by ordering 1,000 *Berberis aquifolia* from Knight's of Chelsea. He bought other specimen trees and shrubs from Toole's of Dublin and Laffan's of Cork. The year ended with a return to tree planting in the manner of his early days. From Hodgens in Limerick he ordered 15,000 oaks, 10,000 spruce fir, 10,000 silver fir and 4,000 sycamore. All of these trees were two years old. He also ordered 12,000 larch and 3,000 Scotch fir, both of these sets of specimens were four years old. Other trees were ordered in their thousands. Surveying the scene in October 1844, Barrington recorded that there were *c.* 20 different types of pine tree had been planted, together with 9 *Cedar deodara* and 63 *Auricaria imbricata*, the monkey puzzle tree.

This work on the planting of the estate was carried out while there was a stand still on the building of the castle. However, in the years, 1847–49, the architect John Kelly of Dublin, working at times with William Bardwell, completed the grand rooms of the castle and began work on the Norman-style keep that contained the family living rooms. It was not until 1853 that a final move was made towards the completion of the building by another architect, Joshua Hargrave of Cork, who also carried out his work in consultation with Bardwell. The grand design of Sir Matthew and Lady Charlotte Barrington, which they had initially dreamt of in 1818, while not complete at their deaths (she died in 1858 and he in 1861) had reached a high level of perfection. The life of Sir Matthew had also been radically changed: a magnificent stained-glass window, erected in his memory in the west window of the beautiful St Mary's Cathedral, Limerick City, and the family burial vault on the grounds of the same cathedral bear witness to this transformation. It was left to his children to preserve the fine heritage that he had created at Glenstal.

The work that Sir Matthew Barrington had initiated on the castle and estate was continued by his sons, Sir William, the third baronet (1861–72) and Sir Croker Barrington, the fourth baronet (1872–90). While maintaining the work of his father, Sir William devoted much of his attention to the expansion of the farm. He was also responsible for the construction of a large stone bridge over the glen dividing the townlands of Cappercullen and Garranbane.

William Le Fanu (1816–94) who designed the bridge over the glen at Cappercullen and who was the author of *Seventy Years of Irish Life* (1866).

Sheridan Le Fanu (1814–73), the celebrated gothic novelist, who wrote the ghost story, *Ultor de Lacy. A legend of Cappercullen* (1861).

The keystone of the central arch of the magnificent bridge was laid by his wife, Lady Elizabeth Olivia Barrington in 1866. The bridge, which replaced a wooden bridge, was designed by William Le Fanu, who was an engineer with the Irish railways. He had married Henrietta Barrington, the sister of Sir William, on 15 January 1857 and the families were closely connected. His brother, Sheridan Le Fanu (1814–73), the celebrated writer of novels and ghost stories, also made his mark upon the area. One of his ghost stories was set 'midway up the romantic glen of Cappercullen'. It was entitled, *Ultor de Lacy. A Legend of Cappercullen*. Standing on the bridge built by his brother, William, one can see traces of the ruins which served as the inspiration for Le Fanu's ghost story — two young women living in their castle home in fear of the ghost who came from the depths of the glen to terrify them.

Sir Croker Barrington devoted much of his time to the development of the walled terraced garden of the Carberys. Heated glasshouses were installed by Boyd and Son of Paisley in Scotland and grapes and peaches were grown in them. Sir Croker was also responsible for the construction of the 'Big Lake' on the back avenue. All of these changes — the glasshouses in the terraced garden, the bridge over the glen and the entire complex of walks and lakes — are clearly delineated on the Ordnance Survey map of 1901. Sir Charles Barrington (1848–1943), the son of Sir Croker and the fifth baronet, also had a keen interest in horticulture.

Cappercullen Ho. in ruins

Glenstal Castle
106

Dog Kennel

The Ordnance Survey map of 1843 showing the early stages of the building of Glenstal Castle, the development of the parkland estate, the Lady Garden and the additions to the Terrace Garden.

He became vice-president of the British Fruit Growers Association soon after he succeeded to the title in 1890. At that time, he invited Frederick William Burbidge (1847–1905), the curator of Trinity College Botanic Gardens, to visit Glenstal with the intention of him writing an article for *The Gardener's Magazine*. Burbidge later became the director of the Botanic Gardens, Glasnevin, and wrote many books on plants and flowers; some illustrated by his own watercolours. He had also spent some time in Borneo, while he was plant-hunting for the Veitch nursery. For all of these reasons, the article by Burbidge, published on 10 October 1891, is of great importance. Grateful acknowledgement is given to Patrick Bowe who discovered this article some years ago. The article reads as follows:

> Glenstal is one of the most beautiful and remarkable of all the country seats in County Limerick, and deserving of due notice for its cultural beauty, as well as for its ancient fame. The place was originally acquired by purchase, by the second baronet Sir Matthew Barrington, who built the present castle somewhere about the year 1838, but it stands on a much older site, and in the midst of a very charming country. The pleasure grounds, consisting of some 60 acres, were planned by the original purchaser, and were formed with singular taste and judgement. Fond of trees, Sir Matthew planted examples of nearly all the choicest of trees and shrubs known in his time, and when I add that his was the heyday of Loudon's fame, 1838 being the year in which he published his *Arboreum et Fructicetum Brittanicum*, it will not seem at all singular that the original owner of such a lovely and sequestered place should have so fittingly adorned it with fine trees. Glenstal is 600 feet above sea level, and the staple soil is a rich sandy peat; in places of a poorer moor-like character, and deep or shallow according

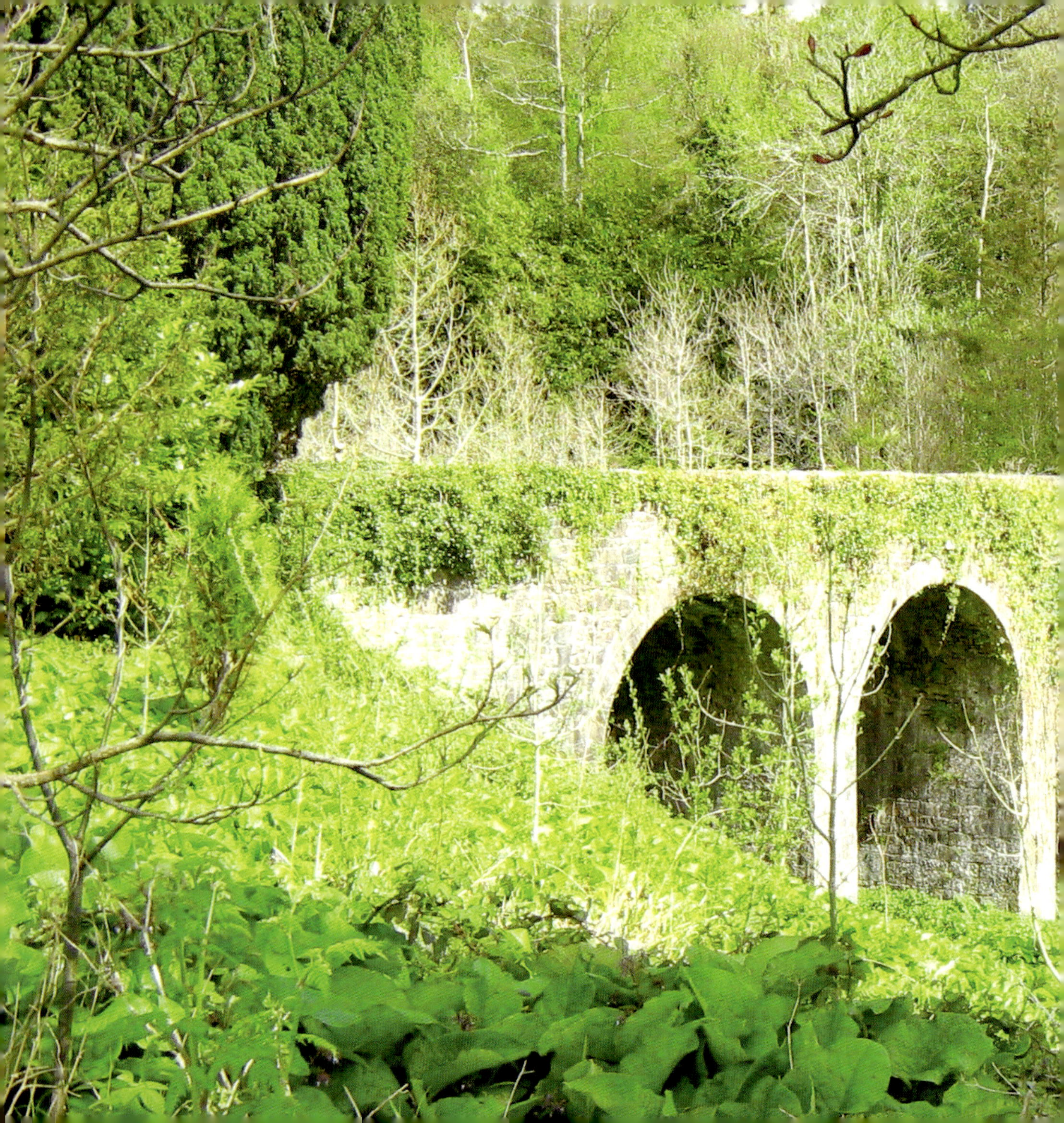

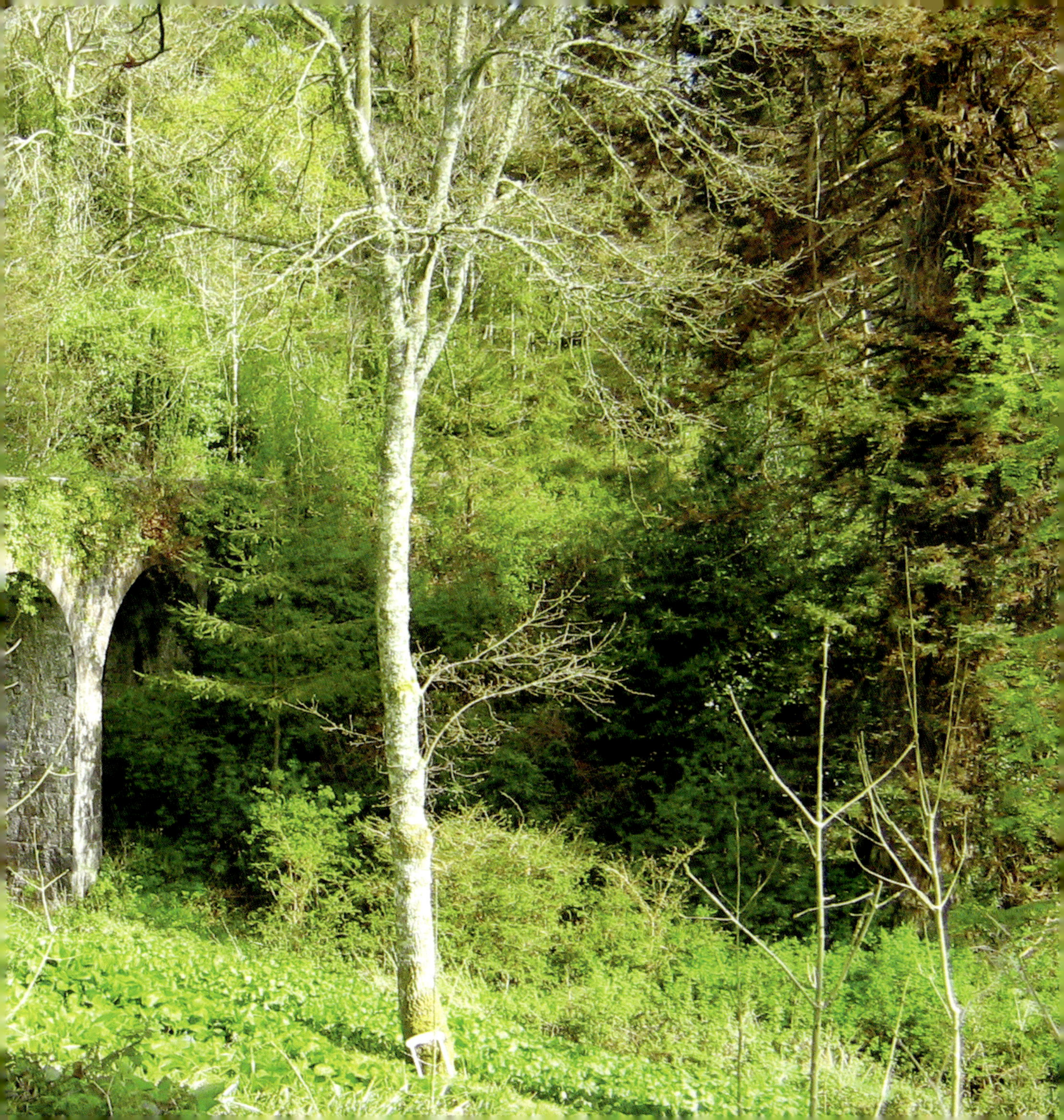

to the geological conditions. The park itself is about 300 acres in extent, and amongst the fine old hawthorn trees and ferns the dappled deer and their young find genial shelter, and a well-provisioned and verdant home. On the other side of the castle a fine avenue extends for a mile, its entire length being two miles, and in the park itself are ponds to which the great winged herons come for their breakfast and supper just as no doubt did the followers of St Patrick, the tonsured monks of century upon century ago.

Of all the naturally good features of Glenstal, and they are many and varied, perhaps the most exquisite of all is the lovely glen from which its name is derived. No words of mine could well or even adequately depict this lovely spot. Fancy if you can, a rocky gorge or valley, two miles or more in length; here sloping and verdant; there erect and precipitous with rocks rising from some 30 to 100 feet and completely draped with ferns and mosses in the most luxuriant and exquisite way. High up above the sparkling water, which wanders through this bit of arcady, tower the grey trunks and foliage of some of the tallest ash trees in Ireland. The beautifully marked trunks of these trees rise in the most varied and graceful lines, here clean and grey or browned by moss, or there silvered and gilded, or bronzed by lichenous growths, but everywhere alike beautiful. These tall ash trees with the common polypody perched high up among the branches do not obstruct but rather enhance the view, and their feathery foliage borne like plumes aloft cast below a most delightful shade. This very earthly paradise is further remarkable for its wildflowers. And here that rather rare animal the badger has his den. It is furthermore one of the native habitats of the Tunbridge filmy fern (*Hymenophyllum*

Tunbridgense), which here and there cover the banks with its cool and delicious verdure. A second glen on the estate, and within a short distance of the mansion, is also extremely beautiful and remarkable as one of the habitats for that rarest of all our native ferns (*Trichomanes radicans*) which is extremely rare, even if it really does now exist as a wild plant at Killarney.

To attempt to paint such a lovely bit of scenery as the glen within the grounds with a pen is, of course, hopeless but Mr George Gordon, the editor of this paper, and many other well known horticulturists have seen this glen and will agree with me that it is unique. To it one might apply with truth the celebrated inscription on that poem in stone at the Taj Mahal of India that 'if there be a Paradise on earth it is this, it is this.' For, in truth, this wooded and fern fringed gorge is a poem in natural scenery instead of in stone.

After Sir Matthew Barrington, the tree planter, succeeded Sir William, a noted agriculturist, whose ruling passion or hobby appears to have been his farm; and to him, in turn, succeeded his brother the late Sir Croker Barrington, father of the present baronet, and to whom Glenstal owes many of its more modern improvements. Again, tree planting was revived, and the fine old kitchen gardens were remodelled and repaired. There are really four kitchen gardens here walled and terraced, and of about 4 acres in extent, and there are well authenticated traditions that these gardens date back for 4 centuries or more. This owner had erected, principally by Boyd and Son of Paisley, the glasshouses, plant stoves, vineries and peach house. Sir Croker also took much interest in the old fashioned flower garden with its quaint ivy, baskets for beds, and climber covered entrances – something like the pleached arbours so common during Elizabethan times.

These old gardens at Glenstal carry back the mind to other days and remind one of Shakespeare's description of 'dangling apricots.'

To see Glenstal in the fruity autumn time reminds one of the nurse's description of her garden in Marlowe's *Dido, Queen of Carthage*:

'I have an orchard that hath a store of plums, Brown almonds, ripe figs and dates, Dewberries, apples, yellow oranges; A garden where are beehives full of honey, Musk-roses and a thousand sort of flowers; And in the midst doth run a silver stream; Where thou shalt see the red-gilled fishes leap, White swans and many lovely water-fowls, Now speak, Ascanius, will you go, or no?'

I thought of this dear old nurse's most delectable garden, when Sir Charles Barrington sent me a kindly invitation to visit Glenstal for the first time. One of the special outdoor features here is the wealth and healthy growth and profuse blossoming of the rhododendrons, which fully appreciate the deep and peaty soil. Nearly all the named hybrid rhododendrons find a home here and the *R. ponticum* is represented by the thousand and by the acre, indeed I believe that there are altogether about four miles of walks here all more or less enlivened by these flowers in due season. Among them is one large group containing about 100 of Waterer's choice seedlings and there are great tree like masses of *Fuchsia Riccartonii* some ten or twelve feet high. There are also great groups of azaleas, hydrangeas and many other fowering shrubs about the grounds. The bamboos are also spendid in vigour and grace. One specimen of Bamboo *Arundinaria falcata* by the margin of a pond is fully 30 feet high and there are luxuriant plants of *Gunnera manicata*, *Polygonum sachalinense* and other specimen plants.

In the flower garden proper, with its noble old cedars, beds of one kind of plant only are the rule and summer bedding plants, formerly much grown here, are giving place to masses of the finest herbaceous plants, bulbs and perennials. The noble herbaceous borders are of the best of hardy flowers and Sir Charles has already begun wild gardening with bulbs in the grass, a feature to which the grounds lend themselves with peculiarly good effect. Here

Watercolour of the front avenue, by Florence Barrington, *c.* 1920.

and there on the lawns and about the pleasure grounds are some coniferous trees. There is a veteran yew, with a trunk some 12 feet in circumference, and examples of *Picea nordmanniana*, *Abies excelsa*, *Pinus insignis*, *Abies alertiana* and many *Araucarias* (monkey puzzle).

The present owner of Glenstal, Sir Charles Barrington, is a keen naturalist. He lives among his tenantry devoted to a country life among his trees and flowers but not without due care for weightier things. He is Vice-president of the British Fruit Growers Association and a willing supporter of horticulture generally and of the deserving garden charities. Under his fostering care Glenstal seems destined to grow in beauty and interest more and more. His efforts in this direction are ably seconded by Mr R. Weller under whose zealous care all things seem to prosper and to whom my best thanks are due for much valuable information cheerfully and promptly supplied.

The Barrington family in 1915: left to right, Charles, Winnie, Lady Mary Rose, Fitzwilliam and Sir Charles Barrington.

The End of the Barrington Era

Sir Charles Barrington married Mary Rose Bacon in February 1895 and had three children: Winifred, Charles and Alexander Fitzwilliam. For many years they led a happy life in their castle home and maintained the estate in excellent condition. He also continued the tradition of his predecessors in developing coverts for the shooting of game. The recent publication by Peter Bacon (*A Social History of Game Shooting in Ireland*, Dublin, 2012) suggests that the Barrington coverts were among the best in Victorian and Edwardian Ireland. Woodcock and pheasants were the main targets of the shoots but rabbits and hares were also shot. Then events beyond the control of Sir Charles forced him to sell the castle and estate in 1926 and to move to England. Many land acts from *c*. 1880s onwards had gradually reduced the size of the great landed estates and made it more difficult for them to be financially viable. The events of the Irish War of Independence (1919–21) and the Irish Civil War (1922–3) had also created economic difficulties and introduced a political system that was not in sympathy with the Unionist ideals of Sir Charles. Moreover, the death of his daughter, Winifred — an innocent victim of an IRA ambush on 14 May 1921 — had caused great distress to the family. For all of these reasons, Sir Charles offered the castle and estate, as a free gift, to the new Irish Free State authorities in 1925. By that time he, and his family, were living in Hampshire, England. The proposal was that Glenstal Castle should be used as a country residence for the president of the Executive Council in a similar fashion to the way Chequers was used as the country residence for the prime minister of England. In the course of his correspondence with Free State officials concerning this proposal, Sir Charles, on 19 June 1925, described to Eamonn Duggan the beauty of the old oak forest on the front avenue and recounted that, every autumn, about 50 packhorses took wood from the forest to be used in the ship-building yards of Cork. In the same letter he referred to the Ilchester Oak thus showing that the story of the marriage of Mary O'Grady to the son of the Earl of Ilchester was alive at that time. Finally, on 29 July 1925, William T. Cosgrave, president of

Watercolour of the Terrace Garden, *c.* 1920, by Florence Barrington.

the Executive Council of the Irish Free State, informed Sir Charles that the Council was unable to accept the gift owing to the financial costs of maintaining the property. The letter of Cosgrave, written after he had visited Glenstal, brings to an end the Barrington connection with Glenstal.

My dear Sir Charles,
Mr Duggan has, I am sure, informed you that I was unable to pay my promised visit to Glenstal as early as I had expected owing to the fact that the Dáil was prolonged for a fortnight after the date on which it was due to adjourn.

The Governor General offered to accompany me and we went down to Glenstal yesterday fortnight. The party included the Governor General, his son Mr Joseph Healy, Mr O'Hegarty, Secretary to the Executive Council, Mr E.J. Duggan and myself. The Governor General brought luncheon baskets. We were met at Glenstal by your steward, Mr McBean, and he, with the housekeeper, very kindly helped to make our stay at the Castle most enjoyable.

After lunch we were shown over the Castle, the Castle grounds and gardens and despite the fact that it was raining very heavily we made an exhaustive survey of the whole place. Notwithstanding all that Mr Duggan had told us about the Castle, we were astonished at its magnificence, which far exceeded our expectations.

It is with the greatest personal regret that we feel compelled to refuse your very generous offer. Our present economic position would not warrant the Ministry in applying to the Dáil to vote the necessary funds for the upkeep of Glenstal, especially in view of the fact that we have already on our hands the Chief Secretary's and Under Secretary's Lodges in the Phoenix Park, both of which are unoccupied and are a heavy financial burden on the State.

I think you should know

Watercolour of Glenstal Castle with rhododendrons, *c.* 1920, by Florence Barrington.

that before making this decision I approached the leaders of the different parties in the Dáil, all of whom, in common with the members of the Executive Council, were convinced of the difficulties, in the circumstances of the moment, of accepting your gift while they keenly regretted that it was necessary to decline so magnificent an offer made in a spirit so generous and patriotic.

May I therefore convey from the Executive Council to you, Sir Charles, this expression of sincere thanks for your munificent offer.

Now, having lost Glenstal, may I say that I deeply regret that you are leaving us. Our acquaintance has been short but I have the most pleasant recollections of it and my pleasure is to a considerable extent saddened by the news that you have definitely decided to leave Ireland. I sincerely trust, however, that whenever you are in Dublin you will not fail to call on me so that I may renew an acquaintanceship of which I have many happy recollections.

With best wishes to you and Lady Barrington, and sincere thanks in which I am joined by each member of the Executive Council.

I am sincerely yours.
William Cosgrave (*in Irish*)
President of the Executive Council

Fortunately, a few years before the Barrington's left Glenstal, Florence Barrington, a niece of Sir Charles and a talented artist, painted some fine watercolours of the gardens and of the grounds. Florence (1894–1968) was the daughter of Croker Barrington and Florence Jane Bayly; she lived at Clonkeen House and attended the National School at Barrington's Bridge; and she then trained as a nurse at Barrington's Hospital. When the First World War broke out, she volunteered to serve in the Voluntary Ambulance Division in Russia during the dramatic years of 1916–17. Although she did not train as an artist, her watercolours, painted when she was still a young woman, serve as a vivid reminder of the grandeur of the estate at that time.

William Bardwell's original design for Glenstal Castle, which was not fully completed.

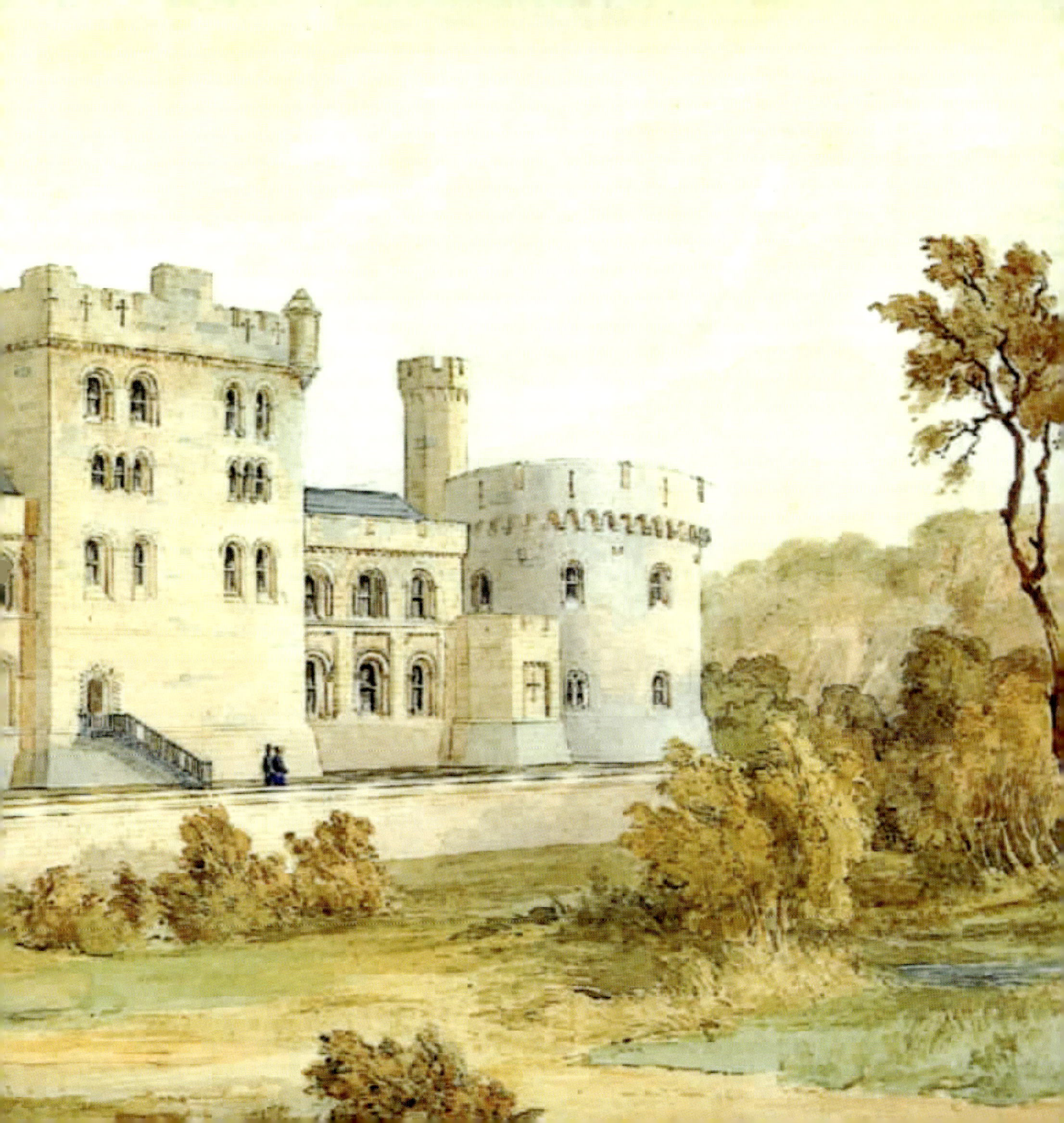

The Benedictine Heritage

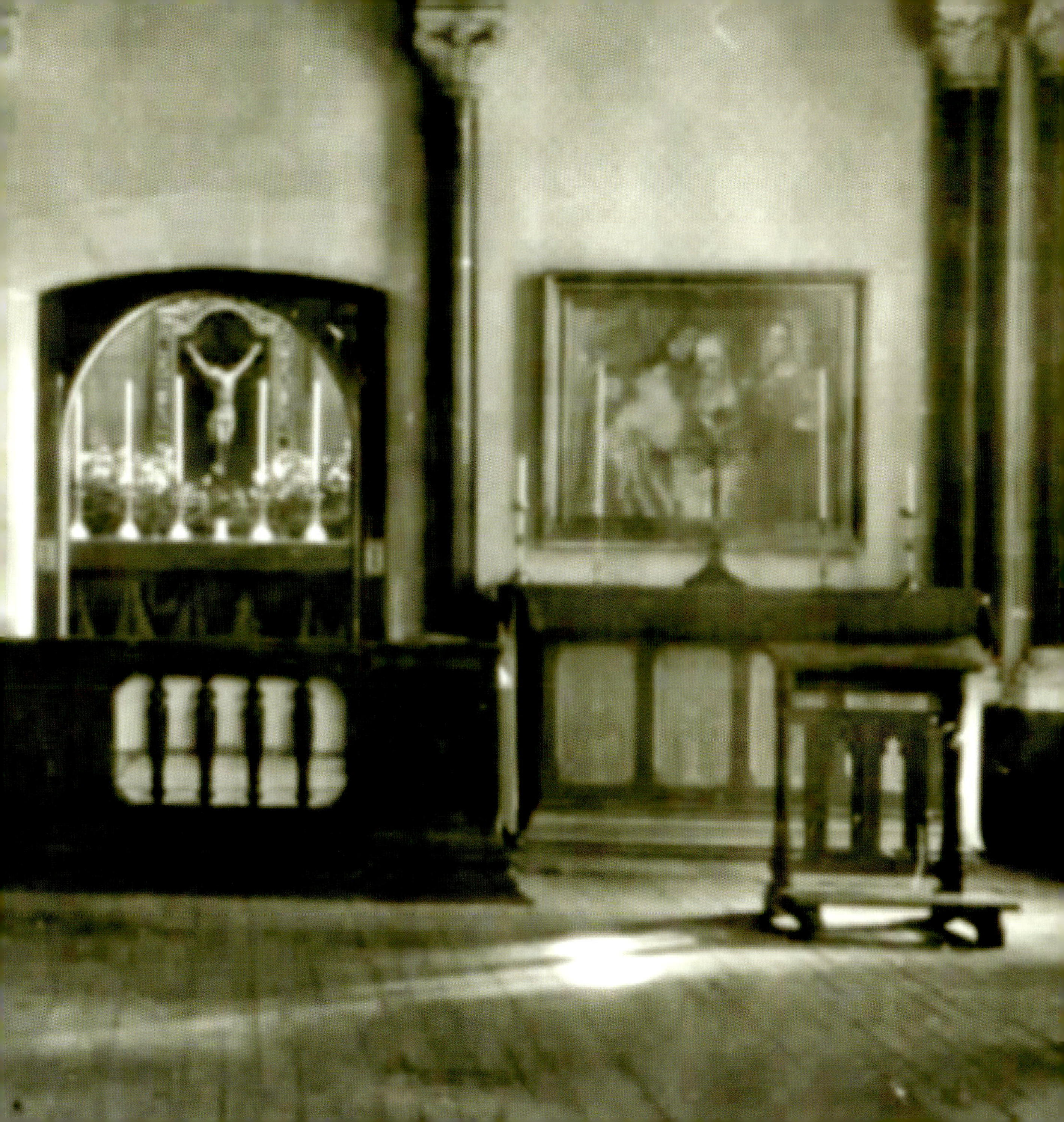

In 1926, Mgr James Ryan, a priest of the Archdiocese of Cashel, bought Glenstal for £2,000 from Sir Charles Barrington. The transaction took place after consultation with Archbishop John Harty and Fr Richard Devane and it was intended that Glenstal should become the centre of a monastic foundation. Contacts existed between these priests and the Benedictine Abbey of Maredsous in Belgium where the Dublin-born priest, Columba Marmion (1858–1923), now Blessed Columba Marmion, had been abbot. Further consultations took place and, finally, on 13 May 1927, four monks from the abbey arrived in Glenstal and began the task of establishing a Benedictine foundation. The monks from Belgium were soon joined by Irish monks and the original small group expanded rapidly, with the result that Glenstal became an independent priory in 1948 and an abbey in 1957. From the original foundation in 1927, until the present, the care of Glenstal Castle and the estate has been in the hands of the Benedictine monks. There were two notable differences between the Glenstal Estate of Sir Charles Barrington and that of the Benedictine community: firstly, the size of the estate had been greatly reduced by the many land transactions from 9,500 acres to *c.* 450 acres; and, secondly, the farm, which had been located outside the confines of the main avenues, now occupied some land inside the grounds of the parkland estate. The original Barrington farm is now owned and maintained by the Gow family who had been the farm stewards of the Barrington family for many years.

Some contact was made between the Belgian monks and Sir Charles Barrington. On 20 February 1940, Sir Charles, writing from his new home at Fairthorne Manor, Hampshire, thanked Fr Gerard Francois for his letter and added that 'it is delightful for me to learn that you have made such a great success and that the old home has become so useful to my country'. His use of the term, 'my country', confirms the fact that he always thought of himself as Irish. Sir Charles then described the view from Cappercullen Bridge in a language that indicates a deep knowledge of horticulture, especially as he was writing in his nineties.

'As you stand on Cappercullen Bridge and look towards the pond,' he wrote, 'there are two beautiful Rhododendrons on the bank at the left hand side. The white one is R. Manglesi and the scarlet one is R. Doncaster.' He added that 'there is also a great rarity on the right hand side — a tall young tree that looks rather like a beech (*Fagus*). It is *Davidia involucrata*, the 'paper' tree'.

Although Fr Gerard Francois and Fr Hubert Janssens de Varabeke did devote much time to the identification of the many special trees within the grounds, most of the gardening efforts of the Benedictine community centred around producing food for the table. An exception was provided by Fr Oliver Quirke, who, in his role as farmer, planted thousands of trees in the 1940s and 1950s and described the rationale behind his planting in *Our Catholic Life* (autumn, 1959). Care of the environment was combined with commercial considerations. In this period, the Terrace Garden, including the glasshouses, was used to produce food. In fact, it was known by the Belgian monks as '*le potager*', the kitchen garden. During

1858
Born in Dublin, Ireland.

1881
Ordained for the diocese of Dublin.

1886
Entered the Abbey of Maredsous, Belgium.

1888
Professed as a monk of Maredsous Abbey.

1909
Elected third Abbot of Maredsous Abbey.

1923
Died on January 30.

1957
Cause for beatification introduced.

2000
Beatified by Blessed Pope John Paul II.

BLESSED COLUMBIA MARMION, OSB

Glenstal Abbey Gardens

▸ The first monks to arrive at Glenstal from Maredsous, Belgium, May 1927: left to right, Fr Winoc, Fr Gerard, Mgr James Ryan, James Humphreys, Abbot Celestine, Fr Odilon.

▸ Two photographs of the Barrington stable area, which became the monks' living quarters, including the kitchen and refectory.

▸▸ Br Brendan Browne who was renowned for the tomatoes which he grew in the old Barrington glasshouses.

that time, many monks, including the first Irish-born priors, Fr Bernard O'Dea (1945–52) and Fr Placid Murray (1952–7), worked in the garden in the spirit of St Benedict that 'then are they truly monks when they work by the labour of their hands'. Br Brendan Browne was closely associated with the garden from the time he entered the abbey in 1946 until the latter years of his life. He died in 1992. Incidentally, the renewal of the gardens reflected the ideals of Columba Marmion who had written, in 1917, that 'I consider a garden as of primary importance for monks and contemplatives. One should make any and every sacrifice to achieve this end'. These efforts at renewal were taken in conjunction with An Taisce.

The inner courtyard of Glenstal Castle in the early years of the monks coming to Glenstal.

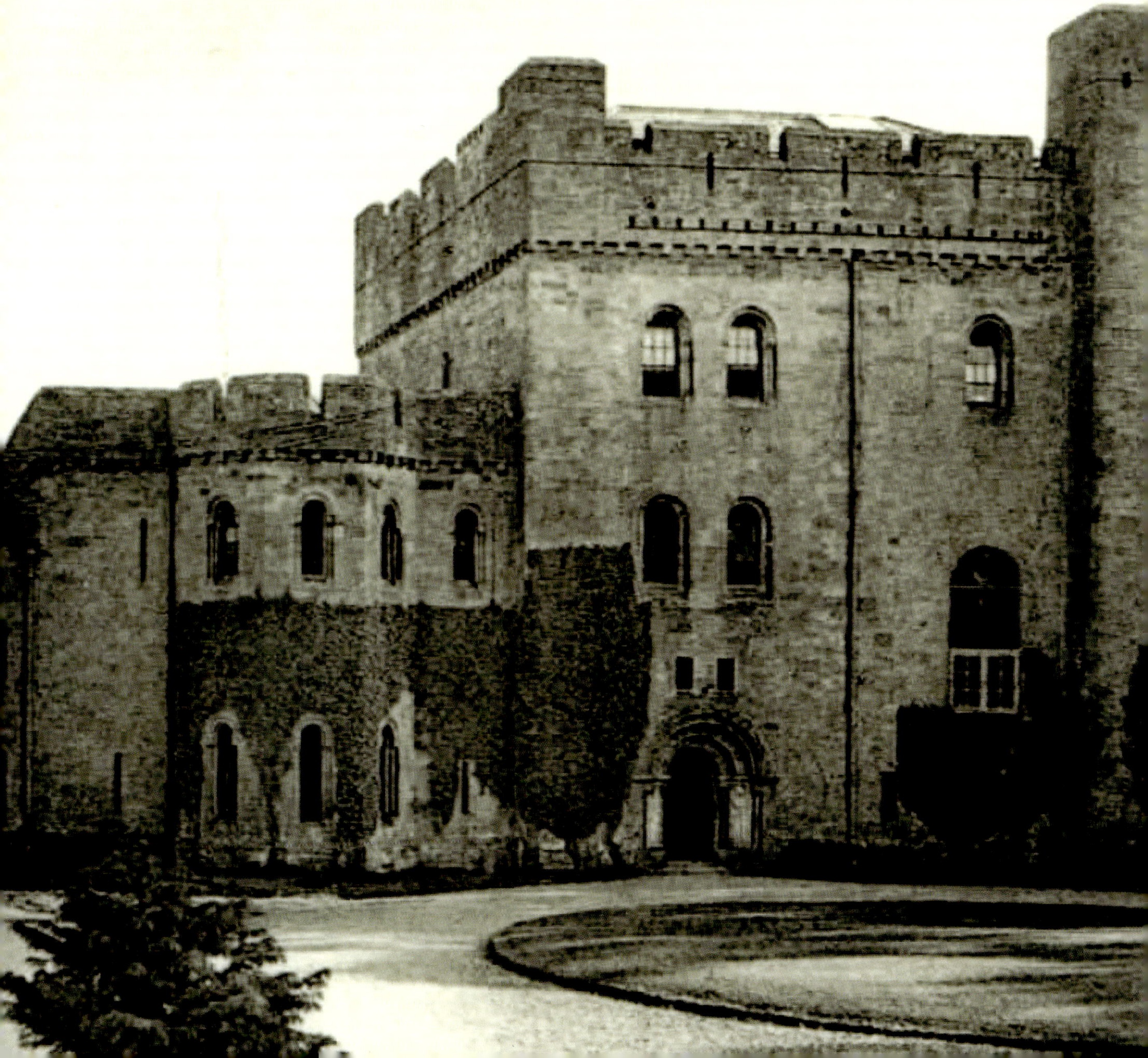

Front cover of the An Taisce brochure (1975) regarding the restoration of the Glenstal gardens.

The Work of An Taisce

Contact between Glenstal and the Irish heritage association, An Taisce, (in English 'the treasury' or 'the trust') began in 1974. On 12 June 1974, Angela Coffey, treasurer of the Limerick branch of An Taisce, wrote to Abbot Augustine O'Sullivan (abbot from 1966–80) and suggested that a catalogue be made of the trees, shrubs and plants in the grounds of Glenstal Abbey. Her idea was that the Glenstal project should form part of Limerick An Taisce's contribution to the European Heritage Year of 1975. Abbot Augustine responded immediately and positively. He was a keen and active gardener, regularly to be seen either with a slasher in hand as he cleared the undergrowth on the main avenues or spade in hand as he planted some carefully selected shrubs. He had been in regular contact with many garden nurseries in Ireland, since the early 1960s, with the intention of enhancing the grounds at Glenstal.

The An Taisce project rapidly developed on a professional basis. Dr Brian Morley, director of the Botanic Gardens, had been appointed chairman of An Taisce's national Heritage Garden Committe and he took a personal interest in the Glenstal gardens and grounds. He visited Glenstal with a large group from An Taisce Limerick, on 7 July 1974, and then made certain proposals to Abbot Augustine. When he wrote to Abbot Augustine, on 27 September 1974, the focus of the project had expanded to take in restoration work on the Terrace Garden. Dr Morley was clearly impressed with the antiquity of the garden and suggested, with a sketch plan, that the walls should be re-pointed and that the paths should be made good.

The project not only expanded but also progressed very rapidly. On 17 January 1975, Abbot Augustine told Angela Coffey to 'assure your collaborators that the Restored Gardens will open to the Public, and that we will welcome their coming at all reasonable times'. This agreement was a necessary prelude to a fundraising campaign and, on 27 January 1975, a draft prospectus was published. It stated that '£7,500 is the target of our fund raising work'. Abbot Augustine also acceded, on 22 February, to Angela Coffey's request that, for publicity purposes,

Glenstal Abbey Gardens

photographs might be taken of the rhododendrons and an RTÉ film crew might make a documentary about the gardens. More publicity was obtained, on 3 April 1975, when Patrick Bowe gave a talk, in the Limerick City Art Gallery, on 'Historic Irish Gardens'. The Glenstal Terraced Garden featured in the talk and Dr Brian Morley's opinion of the garden also received prominence. He wrote that 'the Glenstal Terrace Garden is the only remaining one of its kind to be found in this country. It is a real gem not only for Limerick, but for Ireland. Please do not let its walls crumble so that it falls into a ruin'.

Following this talk, Dr Brian Morley arranged with Abbot Augustine for some selected members of the Heritage Garden Committee to visit Glenstal on 25 April. The group was made up of the earl of Rosse, Dr Brian Morley, Roderic More O'Ferrall and Richard Stapleton. After the visit, on 18 June 1975, Brian Morley detailed a programme of work to be carried out on the Terrace Garden and stressed that any remaining glasshouses should be removed. They were not compatible with 'a reconstruction of a period garden'. The removal of the glasshouses brought to an end the work of Brother Brendan Browne who, for many years, took great delight in growing tomatoes in them. In October 1975, Brian Morley left Ireland to take up an appointment at the Adelaide Botanic Gardens, Australia. He had, however, completed a 'List of Plantings at Glenstal Abbey' before he departed. The list included plants and trees, together with a detailed list of 'The Flora of the Glen' which had been compiled by Raymond Glynn the month before. Glynn's list made mention not only of the canopy of the glen but also of the ground layer and the ferns.

On 10 and 11 May 1977, J.F. Durand and C.P. Kelly of the John F. Kennedy Park not only identified the specimen trees on the estate, some 75 in all, but also located them in relation to the Ordnance Survey map. Some of the trees remain: notably the Californian Redwood (*Sequoia sempervirens*) near the bridge over Cappercullen Glen; the English

'THE PEOPLE BEHIND THE SCENES'

Mr. George Barrer, Chairman, Limerick Flower and Garden Club
Mr. Patrick Bowe, Architect, An Taisce Headquarters Heritage Gardens Sub-Committee
Mr. Sean Browne, Regional Tourism Manager, Mid-Western Regional Tourism Organisation
Mr. Patrick Cleere, Chairman, Limerick County Federation, Muintir na Tire
Mrs. Angela Coffey, Honorary Treasurer, An Taisce, Limerick
Mr. Joseph L. Dundon, Member, An Taisce, Limerick
The Dowager Countess of Dunraven, Member, An Taisce Limerick Executive Committee
Mr. Patrick Fitzgerald, Chairman, Murroe Community Council
Mr. E. Garret Gill, S'.C., Member, An Taisce Headquarters Heritage Gardens Sub-Committee
The Hon. Desmond Guinness, Member, An Taisce Headquarters Heritage Gardens Sub-Committee
Mrs. Mairead Henley, Member, Cork Flower Club and Taisce HQ Heritage Gardens Sub-Committee
Mr. Noel Hogan, Engineer, Limerick County Council and Member An Taisce Limerick Executive
Mr. Patrick Hourigan, Chairman, Limerick Branch, Irish Creamery Milk Suppliers' Association
Mr. Richard Kennedy, Chairman, Limerick Federation of Macra na Feirme
Dr. J. G. D. Lamb, Chief Horticultural Research Officer, An Foras Taluntais and Member, An Taisce Headquarters Heritage Gardens Sub-Committee
Mr. Frank Lyddy, Member, The National Monuments Advisory Council
Mr. S. F. Maskell, ARIBA, AILA, Landscape Architect and Member, An Taisce Headquarters Heritage Gardens Sub-Committee
Mr. Roderic More O'Ferrall, Member, An Taisce Headquarters Heritage Gardens Sub-Committee
Dr. Brian Morley, Taxonomist, The National Botanical Gardens, and Honorary Secretary, An Taisce Headquarters Heritage Gardens Sub-Committee
Miss Nuala O'Carroll, Member, An Taisce, Limerick
Mrs. Mary O'Connor, President, Limerick Federation of the Irish Countrywomen's Assocn.
Mr. Denis O'Malley, Hon. Secretary, Murroe Community Council
Dr. Sarah O'Malley, President, The Thomond Archaeological Society
Rt. Rev. Dom Augustine O'Sullivan, OSB, Abbot, St. Columba's Abbey, Glenstal, Murroe
Lt. Col. John Phelan, Hon. Treasurer, The International Rural Association
Mrs. Frances Quillinan, Architect, Limerick Corporation and Member, Limerick Executive An Taisce
The Earl of Rosse, Chairman, An Taisce HQ Heritage Gardens Sub-Committee
Miss Sheila Scott, Honorary Secretary, An Taisce, Limerick
Mr. Ralph Walker, MA, LLB, President, The Royal Horticultural Society and Member, An Taisce Headquarters Heritage Gardens Sub-Committee
Mr. Robert Walpole, Member, An Taisce Headquarters Heritage Gardens Sub-Committee

End cover of the An Taisce brochure regarding Glenstal gardens, which lists many of those who helped with the restoration project.

oak (*Quercus robur*), with its great canopy, near the school car park; and the Spanish chestnut (*Castanea sativa*) near the path outside the Terrace Garden. In the compilation of this list, they were assisted by an earlier survey by M. Fitzpatrick in 1933, which had been published in the *Scientific Proceedings of the Royal Dublin Society*, volume 20, new series number 41. This article had been used by Fr Hubert in his own attempt to draw up a list of the specimen trees of Glenstal. Attempts were made to measure the height and girth of the trees and to make this information available in sign form to visitors, while they were walking in the parkland estate. This part of the plan, however, was never brought to fruition.

In the absence of Brian Morley,

Abbot Augustine O'Sullivan standing in the renovated remains of the glasshouse in the late 1980s. He was a great supporter of the work of Angela Coffey and An Taisce. This photograph was taken on his return to Ireland from Nigeria where he was the Superior of our Priory at Ewu and where he died in 1999.

Angela Coffey was responsible for taking the practical steps to restore the Terrace Garden; that is to say she became responsible for contacting the contractors assigned to renew the walls and the horticulturists chosen to provide the trees and plants. She carried out this task with great competence and efficiency, although, on one occasion, she was forced to remind one supplier that 'even the most saintly are limited in patience, and we feel we have been on the roundabouts now rather longer than it is fair to ask'. On 20 October 1976, the Mid-Western Regional Tourism Organisation made a grant of £1,500 towards the completion of the restoration work.

Abbot Augustine responded by confirming that the gardens would be open to the public and added that photographs of them might be used in publicity brochures. In June 1977, Dr Durand also supplied a list of plants for a late seventeenth century garden from John Evelyn's *Kalendarium Hortense: The Gardener's Almanac* of 1679. This list was designed to help with an appropriate planting of the garden.

The final plan for the restoration of the Terrace Garden, both in regard to the pathways and the planting, was never completed. However, the work carried out by An Taisce not only preserved the ancient structure of the garden but also enhanced its appearance for future visitors.

In the years following the work of An Taisce various members of the Glenstal community worked on specific areas of the Terrace Garden and orchard. Br Colman Hingerty cultivated a large area of rhubarb in the lower terrace and Fr Gerard McGinty carried out a new planting in the upper orchard. Br Finian had renewed the apple trees in one half of the orchard in previous years.

The First Stage of Restoration, 1986–2004

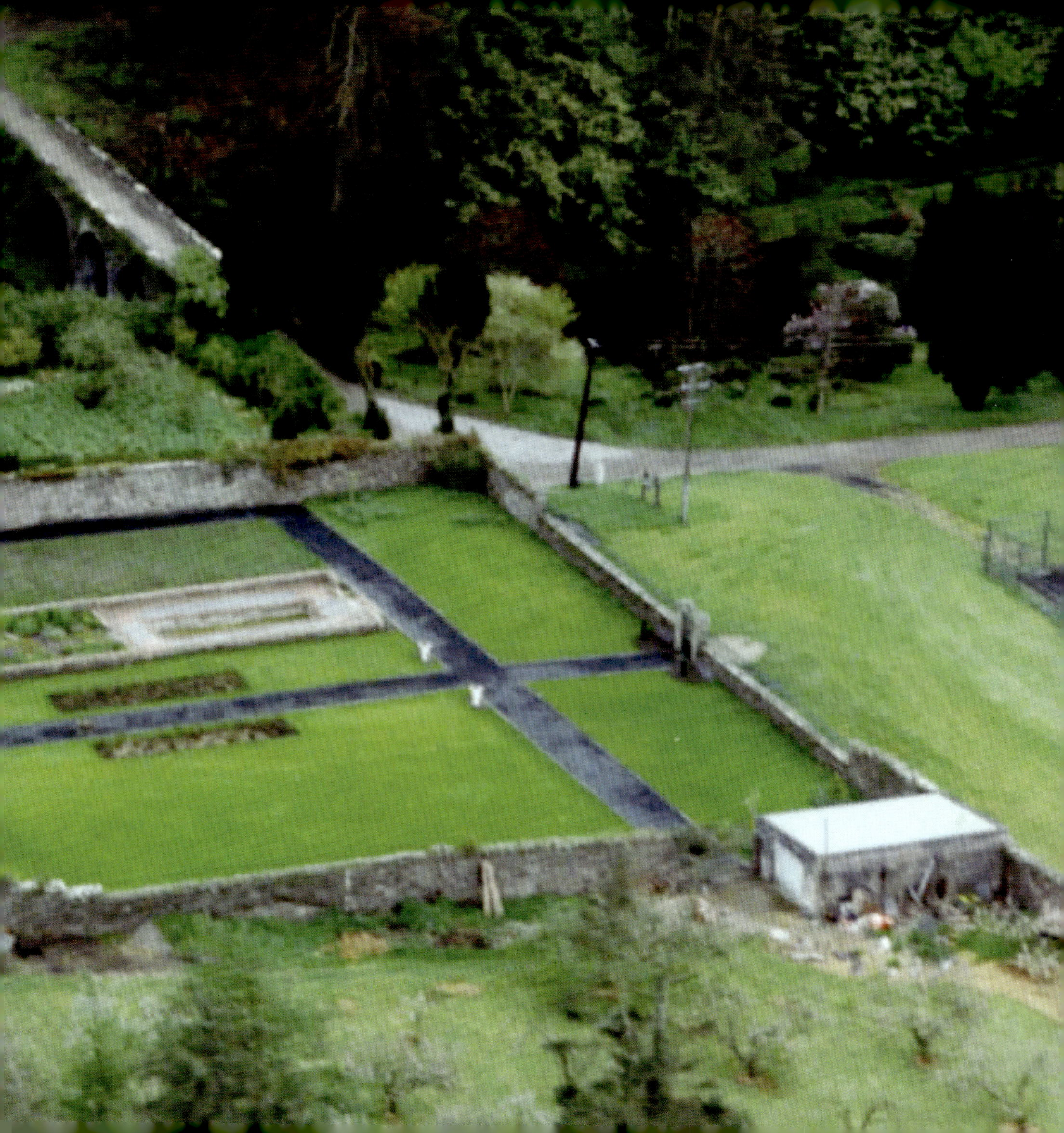

When I began to work in the Terrace Garden in 1986, the condition had deteriorated dramatically. The paths that An Taisce had restored were still sound but the remains of the greenhouses were overgrown. Wild grasses and weeds had taken over all the terraces, apart from the space around a few fruit bushes on the second terrace. One visitor to the gardens, at that time, expressed the opinion that the only option was to let a flock of sheep have the run of the place! Fortunately, Br Colman Hingerty had preserved all the correspondence with An Taisce and I was guided by this in the restoration work. I was also helped by Fr Patrick Fintan Lyons, who was responsible for the orchard, and by Fr David Conlon. Some boys in the school, notably Peter Lyons, Corrie MacNamara and David Kyle, also provided great help throughout their entire school careers. Peter Lyons was of special assistance to Tom Holmes (Senior, 1924–2012) when, in *c.* 1990, an arch was added to the entrance to the orchard. Peter brought many stones from the ruined walls outside the garden and lifted them up to Tom on the scaffold. I recall distinctly the reply that Tom gave to me when I enquired as to the shape of the arch that he would construct. He pointed to the old entrance arch to the garden, which stands at the end of the pathway leading to the orchard entrance, and replied that he would copy it. This he did so competently that most visitors to the garden think that both arches were built at the same time. Tom had set some 30,000 slates on the roof of the abbey church in the early 1950s and this archway was the last work of a distinguished career.

Soon after I began the restoration work, I was greatly helped by the 'men of the roads'. This term was used to describe men who were literally living rough or who were living in welfare accommodation. While living with us, they lived in a small hostel on the grounds and were cared for by Fathers Francis and John. From various backgrounds and experiences, they combined to make a major contribution to the restoration work not only of the Terrace Garden but also of the

The condition of the Terrace Garden before the restoration work began in 1986.

The condition of the lower terrace in the Terrace Garden in 1986 showing the white plaster on the wall of one of the former glass houses. This plaster was removed during the restoration.

Glenstal Abbey Gardens

Early restoration work on the approach to the orchard (1987) but also showing the need to restore the wall and erect a gate to the orchard.

The arch, constructed by Tom Holmes (Senior), and the new gate leading to the orchard, *c.* 1990.

Lady Garden and other areas of the estate. Their names evoke memories of honest endeavour amidst the turmoil of life. Among them were Martin, Tony, Tony M. 'the golden trowel', Declan, Joe, Tom, Gerry, Sean, 'Kerry' Dave, 'Donegal' Jim, Denis and many more. All worked hard; some with great skill; and some brought to the task rare insights of illumination. I recall one wet day working away in a corner of the garden with 'Donegal' Jim, when we were greeted by a suitably dressed monsignor who sympathised with us for the tough working conditions. Jim replied instantly: *'dum spiro spero'*. The monsignor was amazed and rather confused that 'a man of the roads' should have a command of Latin. The words were the motto of a landlord in Donegal and Jim, who had a university degree, had no difficulty in remembering them. The phrase, itself, means 'while I breathe, I hope' and I often recall it as a focus to live in the present and to be thankful. Indeed, I find it is a helpful mantra to have in one's head, at any time, especially when life is challenging. It is also, incidentally, the motto of the Anaesthetist Society of Ireland!

'Donegal' Jim also made an interesting observation in regard to the palm trees that I later planted in the garden. I planted them to illustrate the saying of the psalms that 'the just person will flourish like a palm tree'. Strictly speaking, in botanical terms, I only planted one palm tree, a *Trachycarpus fortunei*, but I planted many *Cordyline australis*, which are popularly referred to as palm trees. After the very cold spell of 2010 many of these palm trees had been badly damaged by frost and two men of the roads, Gerry and Tom, began cutting them back to encourage growth in the future. Jim encouraged them in their work by reading a passage from the book of Job, which predicted that new life would come from the roots of a dead tree, if it was cut down. The prophetic words of Job are now recognised as good gardening advice and, sure enough, new life came from the base of the cordylines in 2012. I must admit that, during the past year, I had taken a mischievous delight in telling visitors that the decayed and dying state of the palm trees reflected the condition of Ireland: there were no just people left! However, the new life in the trees enables one to give the more positive message that 'the just person will flourish like a palm tree' and that thought should encourage us all.

Another man, who stayed on only one occasion, came down to work in the garden with two or three others. Just as we were starting on the task of weeding around the rhubarb, he asked if there was any chance that Judas Iscariot could be in heaven. The others laughed and told him to forget about it. Some minutes later, he put the same question to me again. While I was desperately searching for something positive to say, the others, once again, told him to get on with the work. At this stage, I brought them all over to see the Judas Tree, *Cercis siliquastrum*, which is planted near the orchard wall of the garden. It was early in the year and the crimson coloured blossom was visible on the branches before the leaves were fully formed and I explained that these blood-like colours had led to the legend that Judas had hung himself on the tree. In the silence that followed, the man admitted that he had always been very fond of asking questions. Indeed, he said that his Granny had given him sound advice on the subject. She had told him: 'Do good and you will be good and you will feel good. Now, stop asking your questions!' We all agreed that

The glasshouse on the lower terrace in which the Barrington's grew grapes. This was removed in 1975.

The glasshouse on the lower terrace in which peaches were grown by the Barringtons. It was also removed in 1975.

this was excellent advice: good advice then and for always, and we returned to the rhubarb. As I pass the Judas Tree regularly on my way to the orchard, I am always reminded of the words of wisdom of this dear Granny. I am also constantly reminded of the major contribution that these men of the roads made to the restoration work in the gardens.

The first major task of restoration was to clear the undergrowth, including a plantation of trees on the top terrace, and to restore the lines of the garden. The next task was to plant some of the flowers and shrubs which had been identified by Dr J.F. Durand for An Taisce as belonging to the seventeenth century i.e. those plants listed by John Evelyn's almanac of 1679. Among the flowers planted were grape hyacinths; hollyhocks (*Althea rosea*); lupins (*Lupinus*); snow drops (*Galanthus nivalis*); geraniums (the hardy perennials as opposed to the pelargoniums often grown in pots); *Acanthus* (bear's foot); *Antirrhinum* (snapdragon); foxglove (*Digitalis purpurea*) and some varieties of roses. Jacob Bobart's plant list of 1648 was also helpful and had an unusual historical connection through King Charles II of England: Bobart was superintendent of the University of Oxford Botanic Garden when Charles was King; and he was the King who had granted permission for the Deer Park outside the Terrace Garden in 1682/3.

In the sourcing of these plants, the advice and practical help of Mary Holmes, the daughter of Tom and a recent graduate in horticulture, was invaluable. Born in 1962, Mary

Fr Mark Tierney and myself standing in the Bible Garden on the third terrace.

Fr David Conlon and myself standing on the second terrace in the early days of restoration c. 1990.

died, tragically young, aged 46 in 2008. During her short life, she contributed greatly not only to the garden project in Glenstal but also, through her nursery, to many gardens in the area. The first location for the plants was inside the shell of the old peach house, which adjoins the western wall of the Terrace Garden, and here a rambling rose still bears witness to Mary's excellent choice of plants. Other flowers were planted inside the shell of the old grape house and a small pond was created inside the tiled area of the greenhouse. Some of the old Victorian tiles had cracked in the frost and were replaced by others of the same period. These were kindly given to us by the Columbanus Community of Reconciliation in Belfast. Eddie Dwyer was responsible for the installation of the fountain. In the passing of time, the pond has become a natural habitat for frogs and we have encouraged this by allowing native Irish grasses to grow in some parts of the surrounding area. Among the particular grasses identified are the following: annual meadow grass, sheep's fescue, rough stalked meadow grass, cock's foot, false oat grass, Yorkshire fog, meadow fox-tail, sweet vernal and the dreaded scutch or couch grass.

The large and overgrown area of rhubarb on the first terrace was converted into a lawn and two beds

The restored lower terrace, *c.* 1990, showing the rose beds and the pond in the glasshouse.

▼

of roses were planted near the central path. The roses did not do well and, after some years, were replaced by small circular beds, seven either side of the central path. The design replicated, in some fashion, the semi-circular arches at the base of the greenhouse and the number seven has, to this day, a special mystical, or even magical, resonance. I remember asking Denis, a road man, if he could help with the project and gave him an idea of the space required for each circle, in which the main plants were to be *Crocosmia 'Lucifer', Stipa gigantea* and *Verbena bonariensis*. Within an hour he came back to me with a reply that showed not only an ideal spacing for the circles but also the exact number of bricks required for each circle! By the end of the week, with the help of Tom, another road man, the circles were in place and I was able to begin the planting. The fruit section on the second terrace was not only improved but also increased by the addition of a variety of raspberries and currants. Early photographs convey some idea of the work that was undertaken. Many of the plants listed in Evelyn's almanac of 1679 were herbs and they were placed in a Bible Garden that was laid out, in the first instance, on the top terrace of the garden.

Glenstal Abbey Gardens

Watercolour sketch of the view looking out from the Terrace Garden by Eric Duhan and depicting two 'men of the roads', Joe and Martin

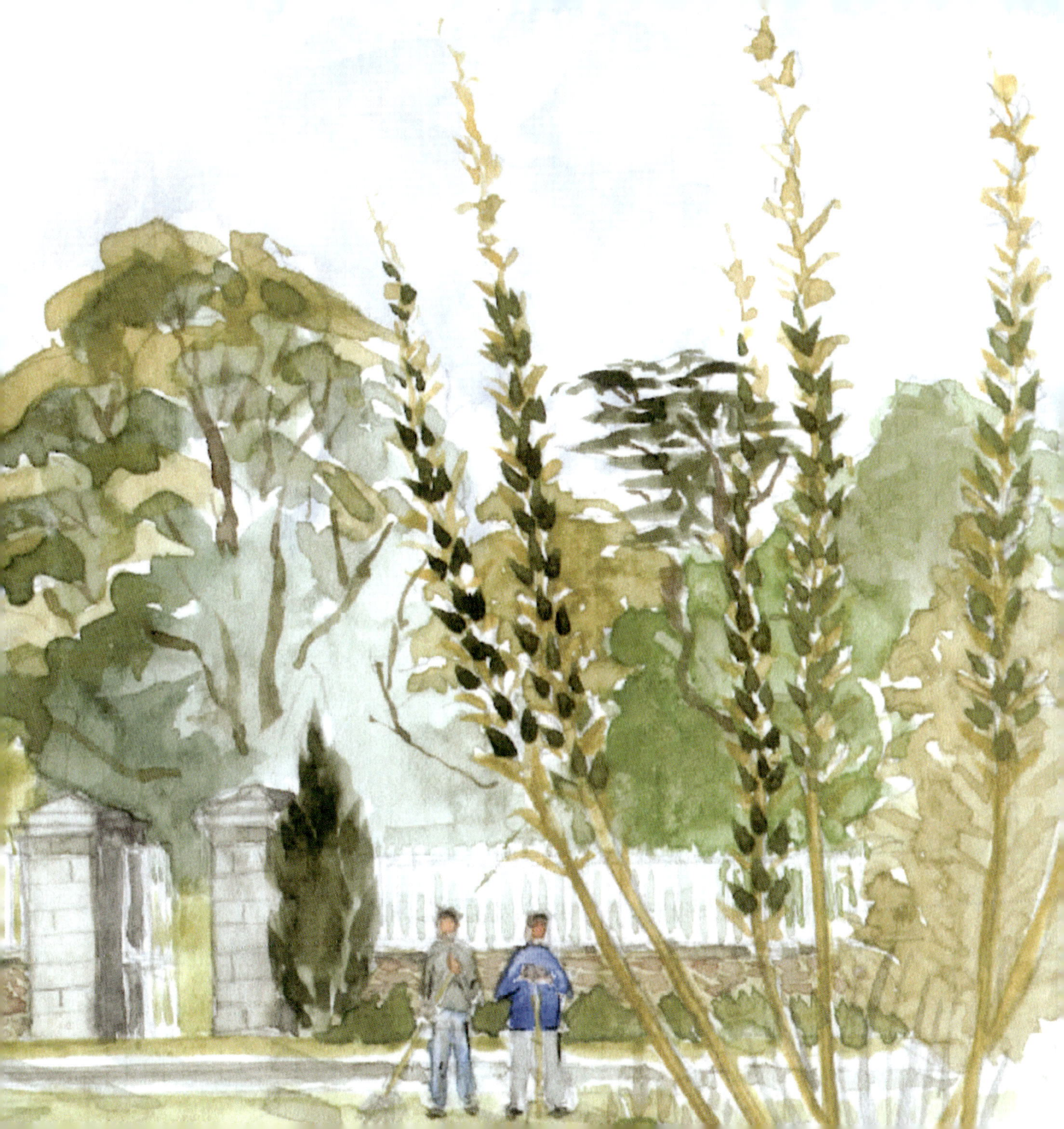

The Bible Garden: Idea and Design

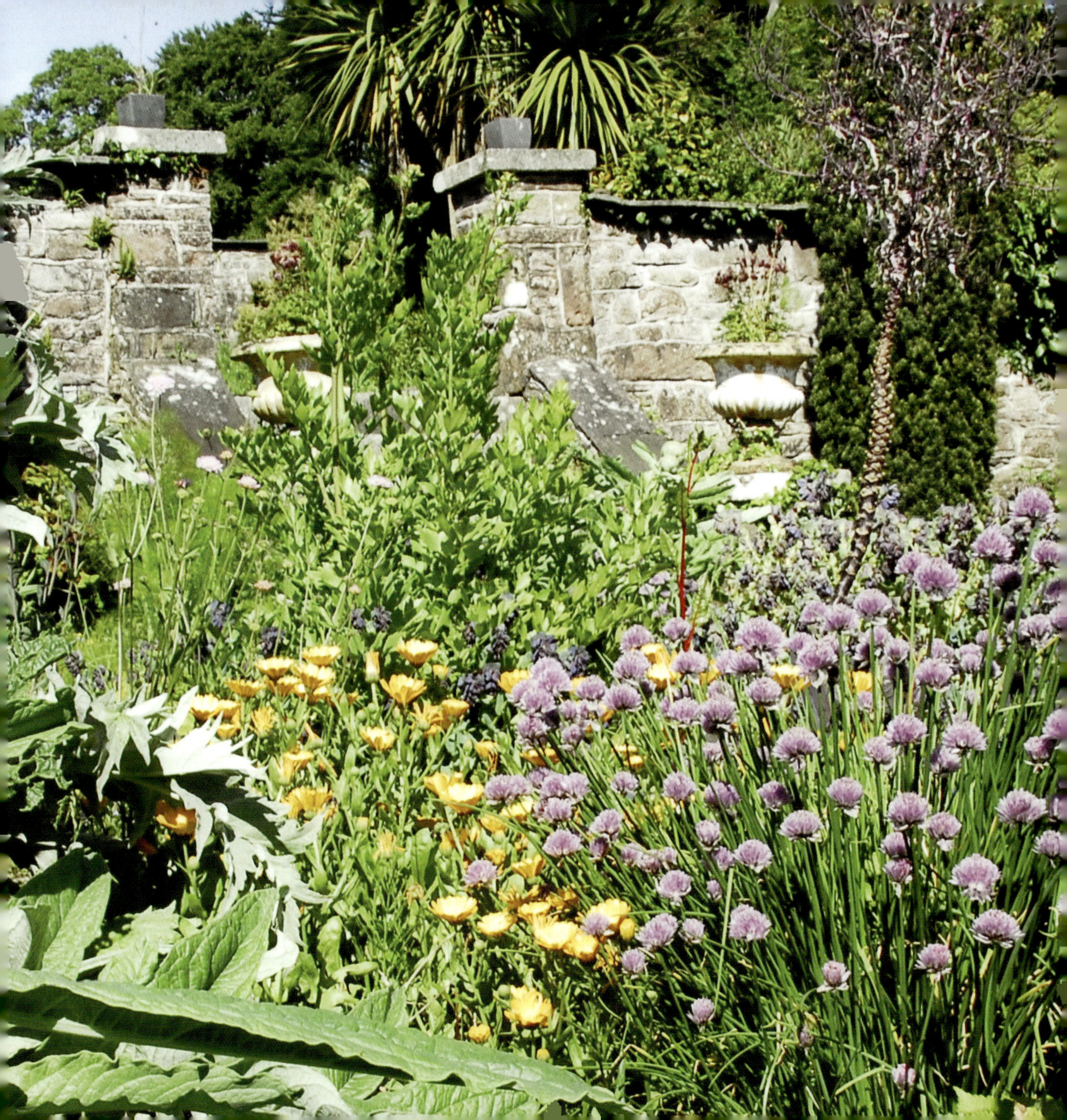

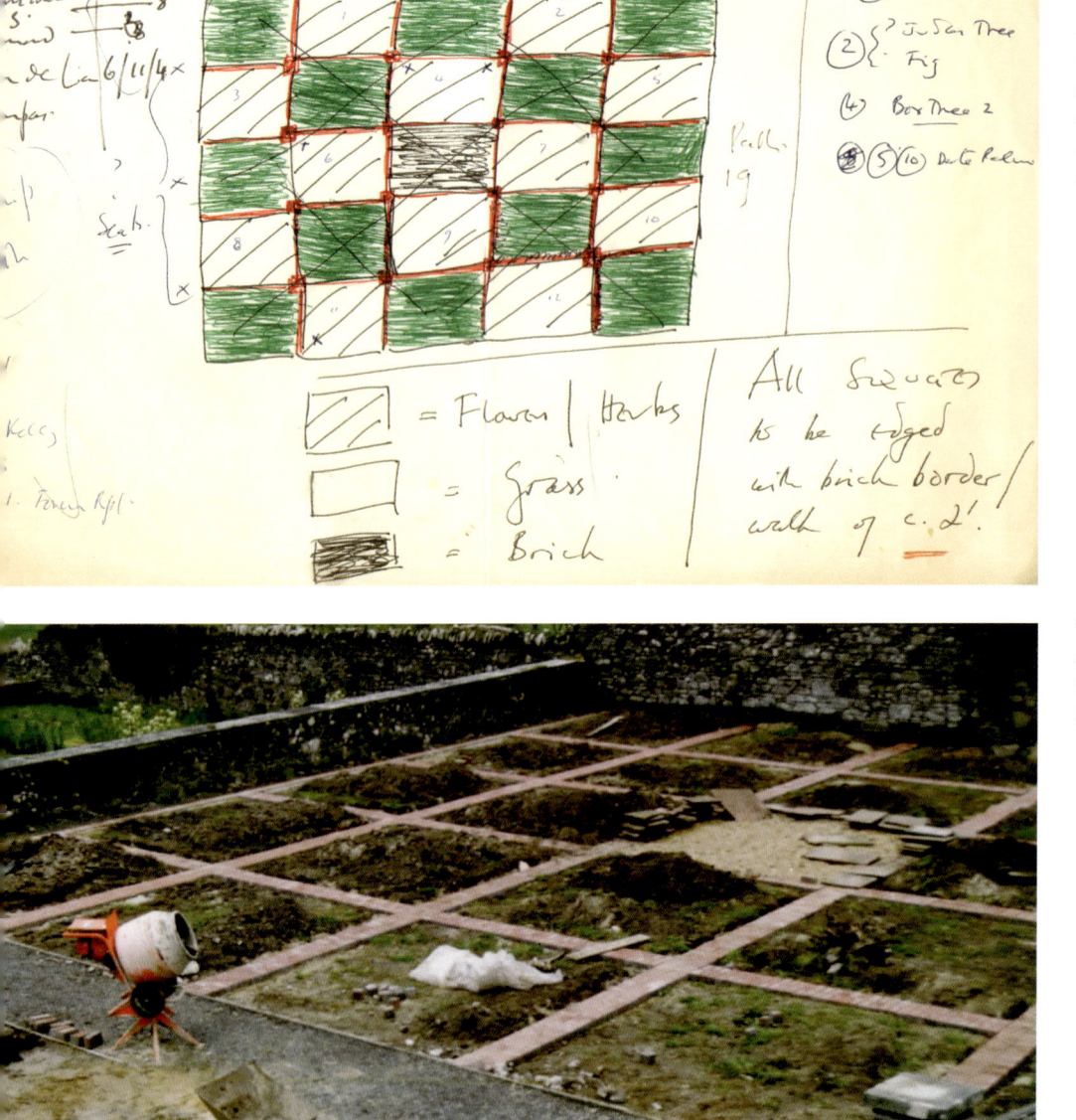

My original sketch for the Bible Garden (1991) showing the chess board design and some detail in regard to plants, grass and stone.

The first stage of construction on the Bible Garden (1991) by Michael Hayes.

The idea of a Bible Garden came to me while visiting St James's Church, Piccadilly, London, in 1989. The church had recently been restored and in the small adjoining garden there were faded references to plants from the Bible. I mentioned this Bible Garden theme, while on a visit to my mother in Brighton that summer, and she made further enquiries at the local library — these were the days before Google! On 13 June 1989, my mother was able to give me the address of Mrs D. Macdonald of Chelsea who had created a Bible Garden for a church in her area. In the meantime, I wrote to Dr Charles Nelson of the National Botanic Gardens, Glasnevin, requesting his help in regard to a Bible Garden. On 21 June 1989, he replied to me and strongly recommended the recently published book by Nigel Hepper of Kew Gardens on *Planting a Bible Garden* (1987). For Nelson, it was 'by far the best (sanest!) book on this tortuous subject'.

Mrs Macdonald replied to my request for information on 12 July 1989 and her advice also proved invaluable. Not only did she provide me with a list of plants but also she added references to two books: Harold N. Moldenke, *Plants of the Bible* (1952) and the book by Nigel Hepper, which Charles Nelson had recommended earlier. She also reminded me of the fragility of gardens, and of life, by telling me that her prize winning Bible Garden had not found favour with the new vicar and that it was no more! Following this exchange of letters, I bought a copy of Hepper's book on Bible Gardens and it became the guiding light for my future work. I later visited Nigel Hepper at Kew and talked about plants and a design structure in which to plant them. A visit from Dr David Robinson, in the company of Matt Dempsey of the *Farmer's Journal*, on 18 June 1990, was also helpful. Not only did he provide advice on the planting of fruit bushes and apple trees but also he encouraged the idea of a Bible Garden.

The design of the Bible Garden was determined by the contours of the ancient walls and terraces of the seventeenth-century garden in which the Barrington family had constructed a walkway above the third terrace. This walkway enabled one to look down upon the terrace below. From this vantage point, one obtained a bird's eye view of the terrace below, that is the third terrace. By chance I had seen a similar view of a terrace at the gardens of Port Lympne in south-east Kent in which contrasting squares of green grass and red geraniums had been planted and provided an attractive chessboard pattern. Taking that design as a focus point, I sketched a plan for each half of the third terrace that was made up of 24 squares: 12 of grass and 12 of Bible plants; and one central square of stone in each half of the terrace. The squares were to be edged with a narrow brick border and more precise measurements were carried out.

The design also enabled one to include two other concepts: firstly, despite the basic use of squares, it was also possible to create a labyrinth-style effect. By walking around the small squares, one could enter the central stone area or sit on the small stone seats that marked off some of the grass squares. In the ancient past, the paths through a maze would have led to an encounter with a goddess of some description; in the Christian tradition, as in the maze on the floor of the cathedral at Chartres, one would have an encounter with Christ. The second design consideration was to reflect, in some small way, the ninth century design that, although never implemented, was planned for the Benedictine abbey of St Gall. There, in the monastic cloister garden, were square or rectangular beds: those near the kitchen contained culinary herbs; those near the infirmary contained medicinal, or healing, herbs. All of these considerations were brought to bear in shaping the original sketch plans and, in the spring of 1991, the work began to implement them. The *Limerick Leader* of 29 June 1991 provided a bird's eye view of the completed construction work on one half of the terrace. In 1992, the other half of the terrace was also laid out and planted. Michael Hayes was responsible for the first part of the work; his brother, Seamus, for the second part of the work. This project was greatly helped by the support of Claire O'Mahony and

The western half of the Bible Garden (1992) as prepared for planting by Seamus Hayes.

View of the Bible Garden (1992) looking from east to west.

Martin Blake. Subsequently, Seamus Hayes has been responsible for the major construction work in both the Terrace Garden, the Lady Garden and their surrounds.

The planting was also influenced, to some degree, by a wish to reflect the regard that the early Celtic inhabitants of Ireland had for herbs and plants. My confrére, Fr Seán Ó Duinn, explained to me how the Christian church had placed the feast of St John the Baptist at the end of June in order to offer an alternative to the pagan festival of the summer solstice. In the pagan festival, the herbs that were used for healing were burnt with the intention that new energy would result from the fire and the interaction with the gods. When Christians began celebrating St John's Day, the herbs took on a new significance. Indeed, the *Hypericum perforatum* that was burnt became known as St John's wort. Other healing herbs that became associated with the festival were yarrow (*Achillea*), plantain (*Plantago*), elder (*Sambucus*) and many more. For that reason, one of the squares was designated to contain the flowers

Bible Garden in the first years, looking from West to East.

of St John. Healing herbs played a central part in the life of the Celts who were constantly seeking to find which herb might cure the ailment of a particular part of the body. This was well illustrated by the tragic story of Miach. He was murdered by his father, Dian Cécht, the great physician of the Tuatha Dé Danann, because he was jealous of his son's healing powers. The rest of the story is told by my confrère in his book *Where Three Streams Meet* (Dublin, 2000) in which he recounts that

> they buried Miach and from his grave 365 herbs sprang up. Then Miach's sister, Airmedh, came along to the grave; she took off her cloak and laid it on the edge of the grave and proceeded to pluck the herbs very carefully and lay them out in order on the cloak. The point being, of course, that the herb that sprang from Miach's head would cure headache, the herb that sprang from his heart would cure heart disease, and so on. However, before she had time to memorise the exact position of each herb on Miach's body, Dian Cécht arrived. He snatched up the cloak and scattered the herbs, and from that day to this, no one knows which herb will cure which disease.

Seán concluded, somewhat laconically, that 'this is why our medical system is in a state of confusion'.

Rather than narrate, in my own words, the planting process that I carried out, I will leave the description to Jane Powers. In 1996 Jane, then the garden correspondent for the *Irish Times*, visited the garden and published an account of her visit in the *Irish Garden* (September/October 1996). Her article recounts the development of the garden and then gives an interesting commentary on the Bible Garden that she found at that time. The account is valuable not only for an objective assessment of the garden but also for the botanical information that informed her description. I am very grateful to her for allowing publication of the article that follows:

Fr Brian, a Benedictine monk, is standing in the Bible Garden at Glenstal Abbey in county Limerick, which he has been developing over the past decade. This singular gathering of plants – the handsome, the humble and the downright peculiar (whoever heard of a gardener cultivating common thistles?) – is held together by an appealing adhesive of biblical and religious associations.

About ten years ago, Fr Brian began to restore the terraced gardens with his fellow monks, Fathers Patrick and David … on the top terrace is Fr Brian's extraordinary creation. 'I didn't have any experience in design or gardening when I began,' he says, looking over the neat checkerboard that stretches across the terrace. 'Medieval monastic gardens had rectangular beds, near the kitchen and near the infirmary, and I wanted to create a maze-type effect for wandering in and out.' Originally, he says, the maze was a quest for a pagan fertility symbol, until Christians adopted the concept. And, in Chartres Cathedral, for instance, pilgrims would come and pace the maze pattern on the floor, hoping to find Christ at its centre. And so the design for Glenstal's Bible Garden was born: on either side of a central path, twenty-five squares were laid out, each about five metres across. Red-brick paving separates the squares, which are organised so that solid patches of grass alternate with beds of plants. The maze effect that Fr Brian hoped for is there, and the grass squares give the eye a rest from the busy action in each bed of plants. Here and there cordylines are planted to give a bit of height and to serve as look-alikes for the palms of the bible. 'I also have a *Trachycarpus fortunei* which I have been told is the only true palm that will grow here.'

Near the entrance, a pair of matching squares faces each other across the path. 'These are my tax beds,' says Fr Brian. 'In the scriptures, the Pharisees put a tax on "mint, rue, dill and

View of the Bible Garden (1996) with myself in the foreground.

A bed in the Bible Garden planted with oats, peas and beans.

Glenstal Abbey Gardens 93

◀ An early view of the Bible Garden showing a 'palm tree' (*Cordylne australis*) growing in a bed of Lady's mantle (*Alchemmila mollis*).

◀ A yellow flowering broom tree (*Genista hispanica*) evokes thoughts of Elijah sheltering under such a tree when fleeing from Queen Jezabel (1 Kings, 19).

▶ The seed heads of a leek (*Allium porrum*).

◀ Fruit on the Fig tree, *Ficus carica*.

cumin" and Jesus condemned them. I can't grow cumin, but the nearest thing to it, according to Nigel Hepper of Kew Gardens, is *Nigella damascena*, so I have that instead.' Another bed spills onto the path with marjoram, fennel and wormwood (*Artemesia absinthium*). Here again the Irish climate has caused hardy substitutes to be used for the correct plants. 'Marjoram – the bees love it – is the nearest I can get to biblical hyssop, which is a different plant from our *Hyssopus officianilis*. When the Jews left Egypt, they sprinkled their houses with hyssop and water to ward off the Avenging Angel.'

The fennel is a stand in for *Ferula galbaniflua*, a plant yielding the resin galbanum, from which incense was made in ancient times. And wormwood is mentioned two or three times in the bible, most notably at the end where one of the avenging angels is called Wormwood. But the sinister thing is that in the Slavonic languages the word for wormwood is Chernobyl.

But all is not so ominous in the chequered garden: one square has biblical grains (barley and wheat) interplanted with biblical weed (corn cockle and thistle), another holds 'flowers of the field' (feverfew, chamomile, cistus and anemone), another marks the liturgical seasons (Lenten rose, pasque flower, Christmas rose), yet another pays homage to Irish saints. 'That was Charles Nelson's idea. Both he and David Robinson gave me expert advice.' And so in the saints' bed there is St Dabeoc's heath, St Furzey's heather, St Brigid's anemone and St Patrick's cabbage.

Another square is concerned with monkish matters: a clump of rhubarb, the old Irish name of which means 'monk's purge' (*purgoid na manach*), is surrounded by monkshood (*Aconitum*), the obedient plant (*Physostegia virginiana*) and skullcap (*Scutellaria*) – 'which

View of the Bible Garden from the side gate in the western wall.

is a mangy looking thing, but I don't grow it for its looks.' In a square devoted to Our Lady, Fr Brian grows blue-eyed Mary (*Omphalodes verna*), Joseph and Mary (*Pulmonaria*), Our Lady's pin cushion (*Armeria*), Our Lady's chiffon (*Levisticum*) and rosemary. During the flight into Egypt the rosemary is said to have given her shelter and its flowers are still associated with her blue robes.

Three tidy rows of biblical oats share their space with different kinds of peas – one of the ingredients in the 'potage' for which Esau traded his birthright to his younger twin brother, Jacob. More Old Testament characters are gathered together in the shape of Solomon's seal (*Polygonatum*), Aaron's rod (*Verbascum thaspis*) and Jacob's ladder (*Polemonium caeruleum*). The Old Testament is a rich hunting ground for bible plants, some with surprising associations. The Jewish menorah, the much-branched ceremonial candlestick, is minutely described in Exodus using botanical terms such as 'calyx,' 'flower,' and 'branches.' Scholars believe that the menorah was based on the wild Judean sage, *Salvia judaica*. Fr Brian cannot grow this variety, so instead he has a collection of different varieties of the common sage (*Salvia officinalis*).

Beds with leeks, onions, chives and garlic refer to the Book of Numbers where the Jews, wandering in the desert, 'complained that they missed "the cucumbers, the melons, the leeks, the onions and the garlic"' of Egypt. Instead they had 'nothing at all but this manna to look at'. Some of the leeks are allowed to go to seed and their big globes decorate the garden in the late summer. Some of the plants in the Bible Garden gain a place just by the skin of their teeth, and often because they have good colour. 'If you tried to be strictly biblical, it would all be very dull. Really, most biblical plants lack colour!' And so in the flax bed

Himalayan poppy (*Meconopsis betonicifolia*). This poppy has not proved to be hardy but the yellow Welsh poppy (*Meconopsis cambrica*) appears every year.

anything goes: there is jolly red annual flax (*Linum*), sculptural New Zealand flax (*Phormium*) and purple-flowered toadflax (*Linaria*). More colour is found where *Crocosmia* 'Lucifer,' the Judas tree (*Cercis siliquastrum*) and devil's bit scabious are surrounded and kept at bay by Angel's fishing rod (*Dierama*), Michaelmas daisies and angelica. 'And I'm looking for an Azalea satan.'

There are many, many more plants in this enthusiast's garden: figs, grape vines and even a struggling olive tree: a bed of pagan plants – elder, ivy, hypericum, yarrow, sedum and plantain – commemorates the ritual of the summer solstice; even common valerian is welcomed. It is related to the plant which provided the nard, the unguent which Mary Magdalen is said to have anointed Christ's feet. But there is one biblical species definitely not welcome. In the psalms, says Fr Brian, 'there are rabbits hiding in the walls of the rocks. And that is just what they do here.'

Undeterred by barriers or gates, the rabbits perform wonderful high jumps to get at the tasty greenery in the good monk's garden. Perhaps they know this quote from Proverbs: 'Better is a dinner of herbs where love is, than a fatted ox and hatred with it.' From *The Irish Garden* (September/October 1996)

The psalm which mentions rabbits, and to which Jane Powers refers, is Psalm 103. It speaks of God's constant care and concern for his creation in images that relate to mankind's concern for the land and for gardens. An extract (verses 13 to 18) reads as follows:

From your dwelling you water the hills;
Earth drinks its fill of your gift.
You make the grass grow for the cattle
And the plants to serve man's needs,
That he may bring forth bread from the earth
And wine to cheer man's hearts;
Oil, to make his face shine
And bread to strengthen man's heart.

The trees of the Lord drink their fill,
The cedars he planted on Lebanon;
There the birds build their nests;
On the tree-top the stork has her home,
The goats find a home on the mountains
And rabbits hide in the rocks.

Psalm 103

In the early days, Eden Plants of Rossinver, County Leitrim, under the direction of Rod Alston and Dolores Keegan, were particularly helpful. Very soon after I began, I also received valuable advice (and plants!) from Chris and Kevin of Garden World (Ellen Street, Limerick). Several specialist gardening stalls in the Limerick market on Saturday morning have also provided invaluable information and plants. Among the most regular helpers and providers are Phil, Ger, Stephen, Mike and, more recently, Eileen and Marisse. Some have stalls under the recently tented roof of the old Milk Market; some have stalls on the road outside leading to St Michael's Church. Many other stalls (well over 100) selling a wide variety of items make the Limerick Saturday market a commercial success and a happy social occasion.

Some of the first planting has either survived or seeded, especially the latter. One can, for example, still see, or trace, angelica (*Angelica archangelica*); bay (*Laurus nobilis*); box (*Buxus sempervirens*); the curry plant (*Helichrysum augustfolium*); evening primrose (*Oenothera biennis*); fennel (*Foeniculum vulgare*); feverfew (*Chryanthemum*); red bergamot (*Morarda didyma*); borage (*Borago officinalis*); catmint (*Nepeta mussini*); chives (*Alium schoenoprasum*); dill (*Anethum graveolens*); heartsease pansies (*Viola tricoloer*); horseradish (*Cochlearia armoracia*); lemon balm (*Melissa officinalis*); lovage (*Levisticum officinale*); golden and pink marjoram (*Origamun vulgare*); marshmallow (*Althea officinalis*); many varieties of mint (*Mentha*); mugwort (*Artemisia vulagaris*); mullein (*Verbascum*); rue (*Ruta graveolens*); several varieties of sage (*Salvia officinalis*); salad burnet (*Sanguisorba minor*); southernwood (*Artemisia abrotanum*); sweet cicely (*Myrrhis odorata*); tansy (*Tanasetum vulgare*); tarragon (*Artemisia dracunculus*); many varieties of thyme (*Thymus*); valerian (*Valerian officinalis*); wormwood (*Artemisia absinthium*) and yarrow (*Achillea millefolium*).

In 2004, Channel 4 selected the garden as one of the secret gardens for a special television series; the other gardens were in England. Apart from taking some excellent film footage of the garden and of the grounds, the interviewer prompted me to give another insight into the planting of a Bible Garden. At the

A close up of some chives (*Allium schoenoprasum*).

end of the filming, as we sat down on one of the small stone seats in the Bible Garden, he asked me to give reasons for undertaking the project. I began by giving the various religious reasons, as outlined above, and then began to recite the traditional verse about God's presence in the garden. The interviewer immediately joined me and we recited the verse together:

> The kiss of the sun for pardon,
> The song of the birds for mirth.
> One is closer to God in a garden,
> Than anywhere else on earth.

Gardening in the sun, or even in the rain, the sentiments of the verse convey a reality which is experienced by many. One quickly moves from the material to the spiritual, from the natural to the supernatural, when one is involved in the life cycle of the garden process. Biblical references sometimes convey this basic fact; sometimes they convey a deeper spiritual reality. Jesus often conveyed spiritual truths through parables and many of these related to farming or gardening. For example, the words of Jesus that 'the grain of wheat must die, if it is to bear fruit', provide an insight into His views on death. Over the years, and through personal encounters, these words, and many others, have taken on a deeper significance and led to some reflections on life.

Glenstal Abbey Gardens

Reflections on Bible Themes

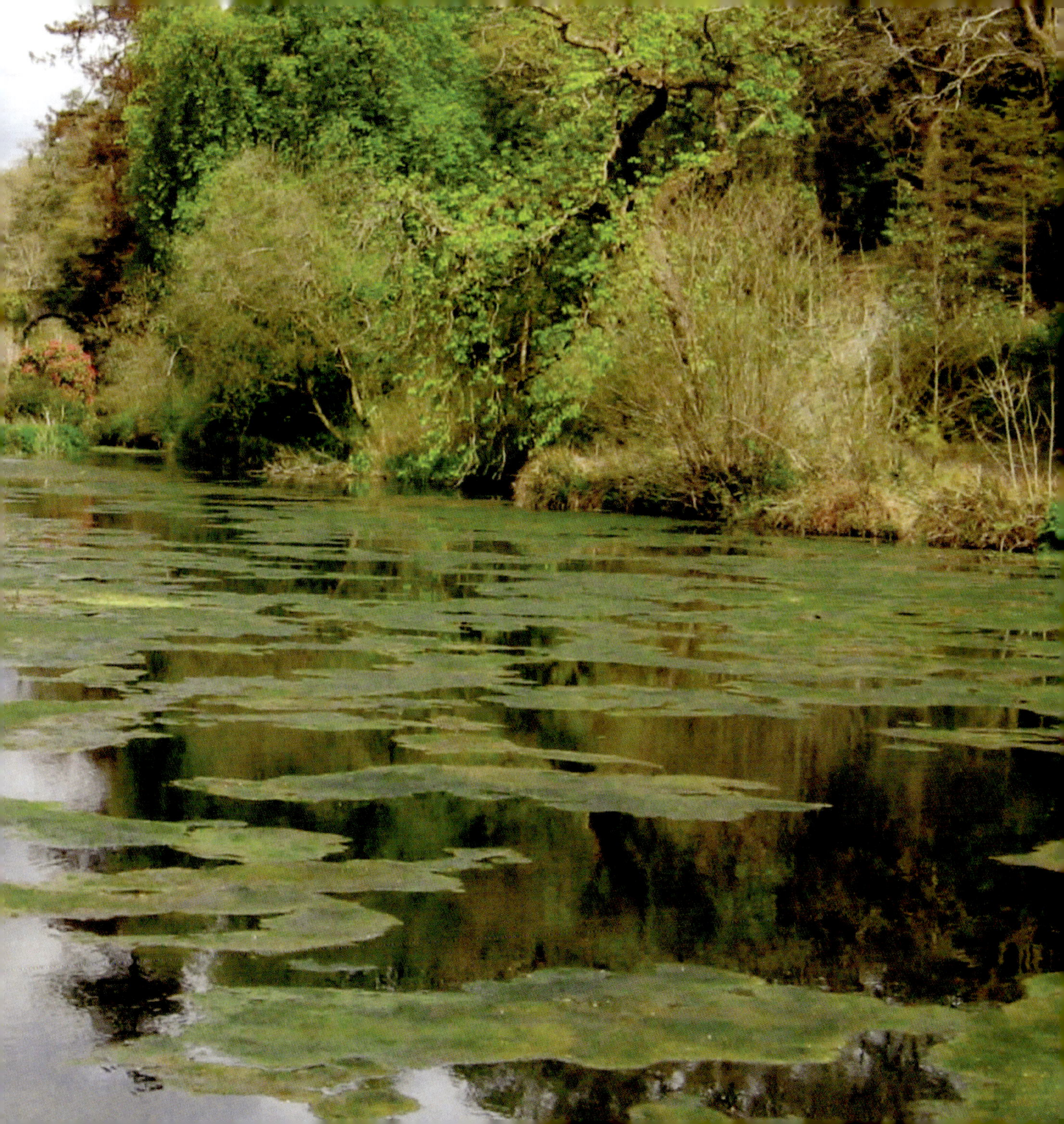

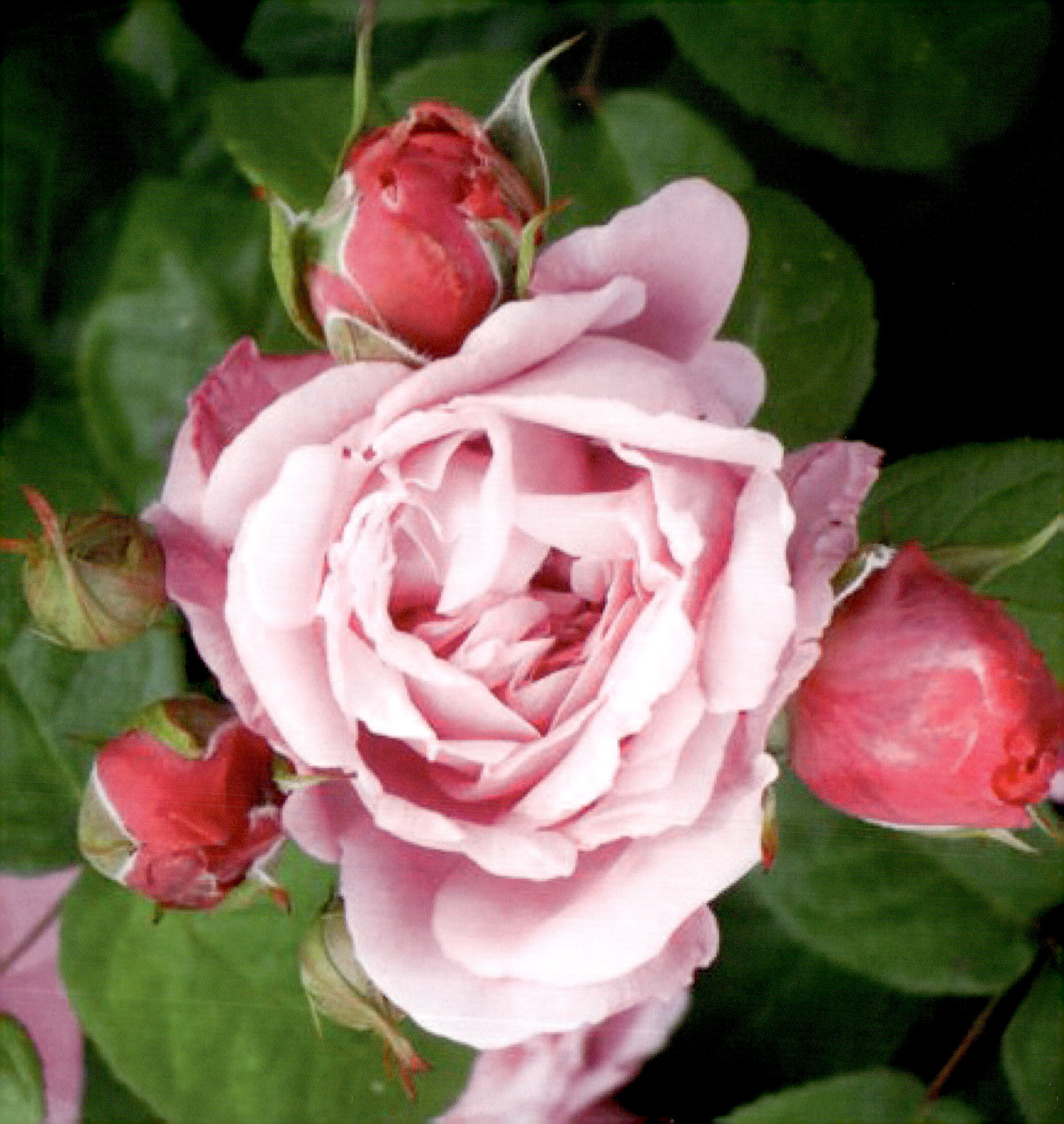

◀ A Mary Magdalene rose created by David Austin. It has a myrrh fragrance and it serves as a reminder that Mary Magdalene was the first person to see Jesus after the Resurrection. She thought he was a gardener.

▶

David O'Leary, Shanbally, Limerick, who died on 20 December 1993, having worked with me in the garden in the previous months.

I recall distinctly a young man, David O'Leary, aged 25, coming to work with me in the garden in the autumn of 1993. He was in the last year of his medical studies and he had been diagnosed with a form of terminal cancer. David wished to work in the quiet of the garden in the few months left to him. One day he asked me to explain the reason for some of the plantings in the various beds and he asked me to explain why I had one square given over to wheat. I listed various reasons and then recited the words of Jesus that 'the grain of wheat must die, if it is to bear fruit'. Both of us realised acutely that the words of Jesus, indeed the promise of Jesus, had a special relevance to him. The words of Jesus offered hope: the grain, before planting, appears dead and desiccated; but after planting it comes to life in a form that is beyond our imagination. So, Jesus tells us, it will be with us. David died on 20 December 1993. On his memorial card there was a poem by Kahlil Gibran. It read:

> Life and death are one, even as
> the river and the sea are one.

Glenstal Abbey Gardens

Only when you drink from the river of silence shall you indeed sing. And when you reach the mountain top, then you shall begin to climb. And when the earth shall claim your limbs, then shall you truly dance.

In 2012, I was again vividly reminded of the significance of the words of Jesus in regard to wheat. The wheat that David saw in the garden was given to me every year by my cousins, the Crimmins family, of Glanmire, County Cork. The previous year (2011) my cousin Sheila had brought the grain, to me in the garden; this year I was told, in early March, that she had a brain tumour. When I visited her in the Marymount Hospice in Cork, I collected, from the family, a new supply of wheat grain, which I planted in the garden. As Sheila was laid to rest at the end of March, small green shoots of the wheat were emerging from the soil — new life, as promised by Jesus, was being born even as her bodily remains were being laid to rest. Mantra-like these words of Jesus — 'The grain of wheat must die, if it is to bear fruit' — have come to mean much to me, when one encounters the mystery of death.

Another such mantra, connected with dying and with the garden, became clear to me, with great clarity, when my mother died on 7 November 2000. Just before she died, I was reading, in her presence, the gospel passage from Saint Luke (chapter 23), which recounts the death of Jesus on the Cross and his encounter with the two thieves who were hanged with him. In response to the request of the good thief, 'Jesus, remember me when you come into your kingdom;' Jesus replied, 'Truly, I tell you, today, you will be with me in Paradise.' As I said these words, my mother died. I was obviously moved and then strangely calmed by the realisation that 'Paradise' was the ancient Persian name for a garden: Jesus was saying, in a sense, 'today you will be with me in the Garden of the Lord'. Here we have two mantras: the request of the good thief — 'Jesus, remember me when you come into your kingdom', which provides us with a basic prayer for all our needs; and the reply of Jesus — 'Today you will be with me in Paradise', which provides us with absolute hope not only at the hour of our death but also at every moment of our lives.

The fig tree provides other examples of mantra-type prayers. It is always the very last tree to produce its leaves. In late spring, even early summer, the branches support the emerging fruit but there is no sign of leaves. Visitors to the garden are often concerned that the trees are dying. It was in that context that Jesus is reported as giving his answer to a man whose faith was tested. The man asked: 'when will the Kingdom of God appear?' Jesus did not reply with a theological answer but simply said, 'when the fig tree is in leaf, then you will see'. The leaves do, in fact, come; and, in a similar way, Jesus was telling us the Kingdom of God will come, if we have faith. At times, certainly, as one works in the garden and sees all the other trees in full leaf, one is inclined to doubt whether the fig trees will ever come into leaf. Then, slowly but surely, the leaves do appear. When they do, they serve as a reminder that 'the Kingdom of God' will also surely come.

The story of Nathanael resting under a fig tree also provides us with inspiration. Nathanael, when told by Philip of the words and work of Jesus, he was still reluctant to leave his resting place under the fig tree (John, chapter 1). Indeed, he rejected Philip's invitation to meet Jesus with the derisive reply, 'can anything good come out of Nazareth?' In the end, he responded to Philip's invitation to 'come and see'. When he did meet Jesus, he was amazed to be told that 'before Philip called you, I saw you when you were under the fig tree'. After this revelation, Nathaniel professed his faith with the words, 'you are the Son of God'. The fig trees in the garden serve as a permanent reminder that the call to 'come and see', and then to share the life of Jesus, is made to us every day of our lives.

Many other examples of plants in the garden providing words of wisdom for us to reflect on might be selected. For example, the advice of Jesus, in one of the gospel stories, 'not to be anxious about anything' but to be like the flowers of the field is especially relevant to all gardeners. Very quickly one learns that plants seed themselves all over the place in a manner that is far removed from

Glenstal Abbey Gardens

Myself checking the fruit on the fig trees. This photo was taken by Tony Rodgers for the 2002 Calendar of Limerick County Council with the theme, 'Working Hands'.

the original structured planting. One also learns that, more often than not, the selection made by the plants themselves is far better than was originally planned! So it is with life: too much planning is not always advisable. The advice, 'do not be anxious about anything', makes absolute sense. Similarly the very precise advice given to us by Jesus in relation to the vine makes for a compelling message. 'I am the vine, you are the branches … if you keep my commandments, you will abide in my love …these things I have spoken to you, that my joy may be in you, and that your joy may be full' (John, chapter 15). The two vines that I planted in the garden do not yield grapes but they do decorate the walls; and they do provide a reminder of the joy-filled words of Jesus: 'I am the vine, you are the branches'. One could go on forever but to conclude with an illustration concerning barley.

Each year, as with the wheat and oats, I plant one of the square units in the top terrace with barley. Barley evokes many biblical memories and one of the most unusual concerns the story of Ruth. Her story, as told in the book of her name, centres around the pledge that she made to her mother-in-law, Naomi. Faced by death, difficulty and hardship, Ruth declared to Naomi 'where you go, I will go; where you lodge, I will lodge;

your people will be my people, and your God, my God'. These words have come down to us as a profound expression of personal fidelity; so profound, indeed, that they are often included in the marriage ceremony as a sign of lifelong faithfulness. The story then recounts how Ruth returned with Naomi to Bethlehem and spent many hours gleaning in the barley fields for the landowner named Boaz. She then married Boaz and from their son, Obed, the lineage of David was created. It was because of this relationship that Jesus was born in Bethlehem. In Hebrew one of the origins of the name Bethlehem is 'house of bread'. My little square of barley reminds me of the story of Ruth and of the faithful fidelity that led Jesus, 'the bread of life', to be born in the 'house of bread'. A truly mysterious connection, which invites us to see some guiding providence behind the choice of Bethlehem for the birth of Jesus. The poet, John Liddy, on a visit to the garden, expressed some of these sentiments in verse.

Stone seat in the Bible Garden with a vine growing on the wall.

The path leading to the Mass Rock in Cappercullen Glen under snow, 2010.

The Terrace Garden under snow, 2010.

The Bible Garden

Our herbalist guide, Fr Brian, explains
The purpose of his plan, its overall design
As we enter this seventeenth century
Terrace garden far from the Lebanon

In Murroe, at the foot of Slieve Felim.
I am reminded of herb shops and musty Basements,
vivid as the stories each plant Enunciates;
their perfumed beds proclaim.

The flowering almond, the last to flower
Before winter's end, signifies fast-moving
Events, our search for answers to ancient
Strife, never ending struggle for fulfilment

The body and the mind a temple of harmony
Not unlike this lushness where chick pea,
Dandelions and endive speak to us symbolically,
Urging us not to be enslaved but free.

We glimpse ourselves in each propped mirror
Against the four walls — reminding us
We are part of this growth but like hemlock
There will be one who conceals a foul odour.

And as the rain begins to fall we incline towards
The lilies of the field, sweet pea and rue
To blossom each side of our homeward path,
Germinate the journey, just and true.

John Liddy 2009

The Second Stage of Restoration, 2005 to the Present

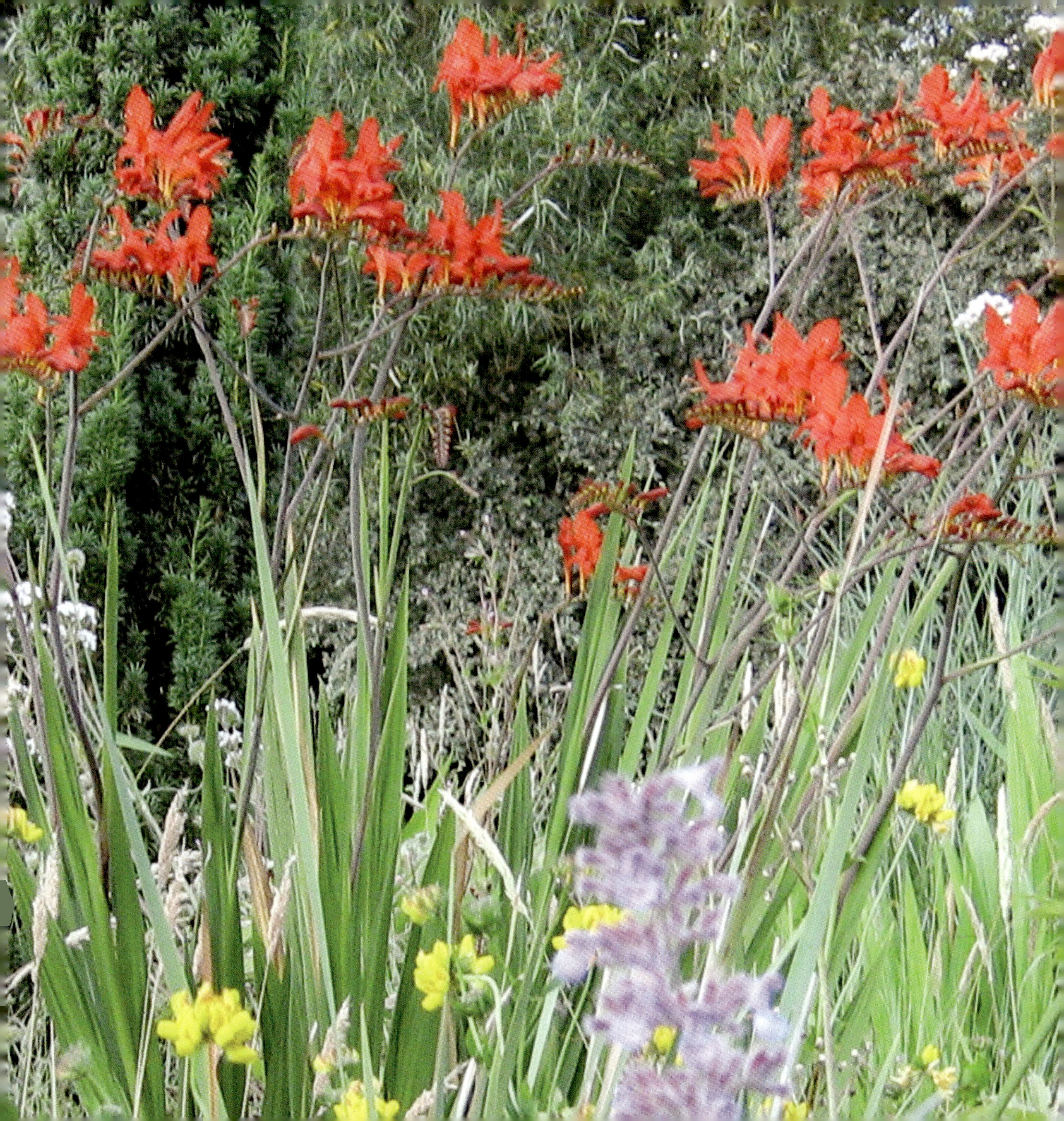

Two developments took place in the Bible Garden c. 2005/2006: firstly, Jacobs sheep were brought into the orchard; and, secondly, the area of the Terrace Garden with a Bible theme was extended. The idea of introducing sheep into the orchard was both practical and Bible-related: on the one hand, the sheep acted as lawnmowers in the c. 2 acres of orchard; on the other hand, the origin of the sheep was directly related to the Bible. In the Book of Genesis (chapter 30) there is the story of Jacob taking every spotted sheep from the flock of his father-in-law, Laban, and breeding from them. The sheep are described as piebald or spotted and, in origin, are from the Middle East. Tom Holmes, Junior, organised the buying of the sheep: one pure Jacobs ram, one Jacobs ewe and a couple of Dorset ewes. The lambs tend to be black or spotted. In the new testament, of course, Jesus calls himself 'the good shepherd' and this image evokes memories of His concern for us. At the time of writing (January 1913) we have seven sheep, although this year's lambs have yet to be born. In the winter months, donkeys are kept in the upper orchard under the care of the farmer.

The Jacobs ram, who has been with us since 2005, whose presence accords with the theme of a Bible Garden and evokes memories of Jacob and Jesus, the good shepherd.

While this development was taking place, the Bible planting theme was extended to the second terrace. At the same time, the ground plan of the terrace was reshaped. The two halves of the terrace were united visually by a central lawn, which was edged with the same type of brick as on the top terrace. Wide borders were created either side of this central path. In these borders leeks, onions, garlic, cucumbers and pumpkins (taking the place of melons) were planted with reference to the Book of Numbers (chapter 11) and the desire of the Jews to leave the desert and to eat these vegetables in the land of Egypt. Over the intervening years other plants have been added to this list,

Views of the raised beds on the second terrace, which were constructed by Seamus Hayes and Br Pádraig in 2010.

Glenstal Abbey Gardens

Cows grazing inside the grassland of the old Deer Park.

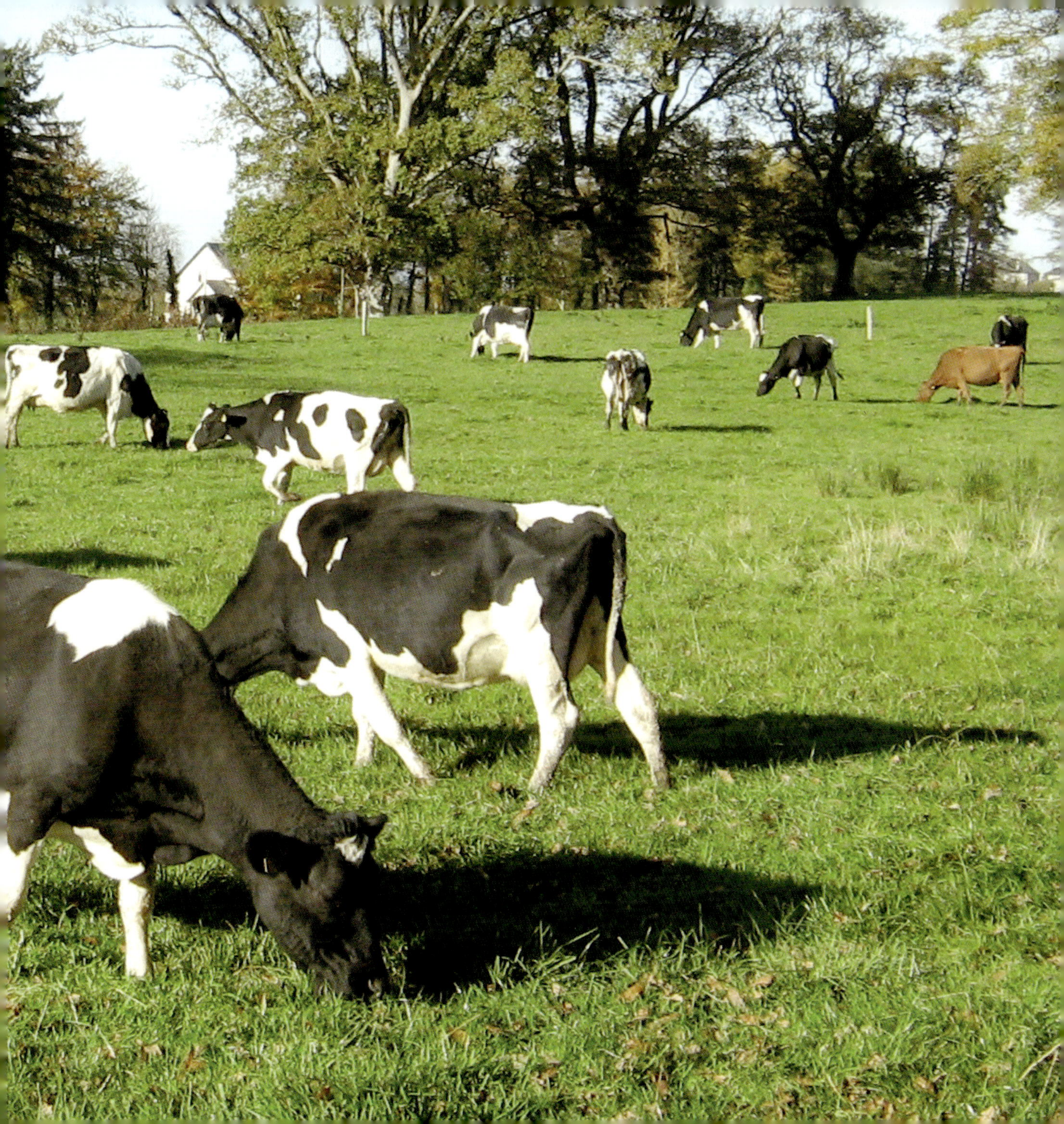

such as decorative alliums – *Allium christophi* is particularly striking – courgettes and ruby chard. One half of the terrace retained its use for the planting of fruit: currants (red and black), gooseberries, raspberries and strawberries; and the fig trees remained on the back wall. In some small way the presence of fruit on the terrace evoked the invocation of the psalm that the 'fruit trees of the Lord should praise the Lord'. The other half of the terrace was given over to rhubarb, potatoes, lettuce and herbs. In 2010, this vegetable area was made into raised beds, which have proved to be not only more manageable but also visually more attractive. Both the reshaping of the terrace in 2005 and the construction of the raised beds in 2010 were the work of Seamus Hayes. In the work of making raised beds, he was helped greatly by Br Pádraig in the major task of bringing soil and manure into the garden. During these years, a major restoration of the wall on the top terrace was carried out by Eddie Prodger, who was assisted by his son and Darren Hale.

While these structural changes were taking place, Fr Abbot Christopher and Br Timothy both began to make significant contributions to the garden workforce. Christopher became responsible for the fruit section of the terrace and also made an important contribution to the care of the orchard. The pruning and picking of fruit has been carried out on a regular basis and the assistance of resident guests (Abbot Christopher is guest master) has proved most helpful. From time to time, the guests have also helped in other areas of the garden. Br Timothy took over three raised beds and has cultivated them in the spirit of our Benedictine abbey in Kerala, India. Many herbs are planted in the beds, some 20 different varieties, and, with the other herbs in the garden, they provided an ideal habitat for bees and butterflies. He also planted many varieties of garlic, one from Britanny was especially successful, and varieties of tall *alliums*, such as 'everest' and 'giganteum'. He even attempted to cultivate a papaya plant that he had brought back from India. This planting was not successful but 'Lady's Finger', an Indian type of marrow, and 'Elephant's Trunk', an

Indian type of pepper, did survive. In accordance with gardening practices in India, several urns, and even a thurible, containing incense were lighted at the start of work and their perfumes filled the air. Feeding containers for birds were also set up and increased the presence of birds in the garden. A welcome presence, except when the fruit is ripening! Many birds visit the garden: the robin, wood pigeon, blackbird, song thrush, coal tit, blue tit, great tit, rook, chaffinch and wren are among the most regular visitors. The nearby chapel lake is frequented by heron and duck. In the past, hen harriers hovered in the sky and Fr Gerard, an expert on birds, was able to identify a twite on occasions.

After the hard winter of 2010, it became possible to carry out more restoration work on the shell of the old Barrington glasshouses on the lower terrace. From the outset of the work, it had been decided to keep the retaining walls of the large Barrington grape house in recognition of the mark that the family had made on the estate. The remains of another small greenhouse, attached to the large grapehouse, became visible, when the *fuchsia* and other shrubs were killed by the frost. Two men of the roads, Gerry and Sean, removed over 100 wheelbarrows of waste from the site and Seamus Hayes, using old brick, laid out the lines of the old greenhouse.

Soon afterwards, the redbrick foundations of the Barrington peach house, on the western wall of the garden, were dug up and then relaid using the old redbrick. The outline of the building is now clearly visible and the bricks look so clean that they appear as good as new. The coping stones, which the Barringtons had removed from the top of the garden wall, in order to erect the greenhouse, were replaced. Seamus Hayes was responsible for the restoration of the lines of the peach house and was assisted by Gerry in renewing the coping stones.

Work was also carried out in reclaiming the ancient walkway, which looks out over the ancient deer park and provides a fine view of the front avenue. It also provides a distant view of Knockfierna (the Hill of Truth) which is associated with

Allium christophi, one of the many decorative Alliums in the borders on the second terrace.

Donn, the god of death and the other world. Martin, another regular 'man of the roads', played a major role in clearing this site. The raised and walled walkway, which was revealed, runs outside the garden wall and may have served as a defensive fortification for the Cappercullen house of the Carbery family.

The fields of the deer park, either side of the front avenue, are now farmland and the management of this part of the estate by many members of the community, in their role, as farmers has greatly enhanced the look of the property. Walking through the grounds, on both the front and back avenues, the fields are beautifully maintained and the grazing herd of Frisian cows, numbering about 100, provides an added attraction. Fr James is the farmer at the present time and he succeeded Fr Philip who ran the farm for 30 years, 1978–2007. Before Fr Philip, other members of the community, notably David, Finian, Oliver and Winoc also managed the farm. They have been assisted by many local men some of whom also worked in the garden. The names of Chris Mackey, Niall Ryan, Tom Lynch, Paddy Rainsford, Paddy Dwyer, Mick Quinlan, Christy Fitzgibbon and Johnny Davis, still working here after *c.* 20 years, come to mind.

The Restoration of the Lady Garden

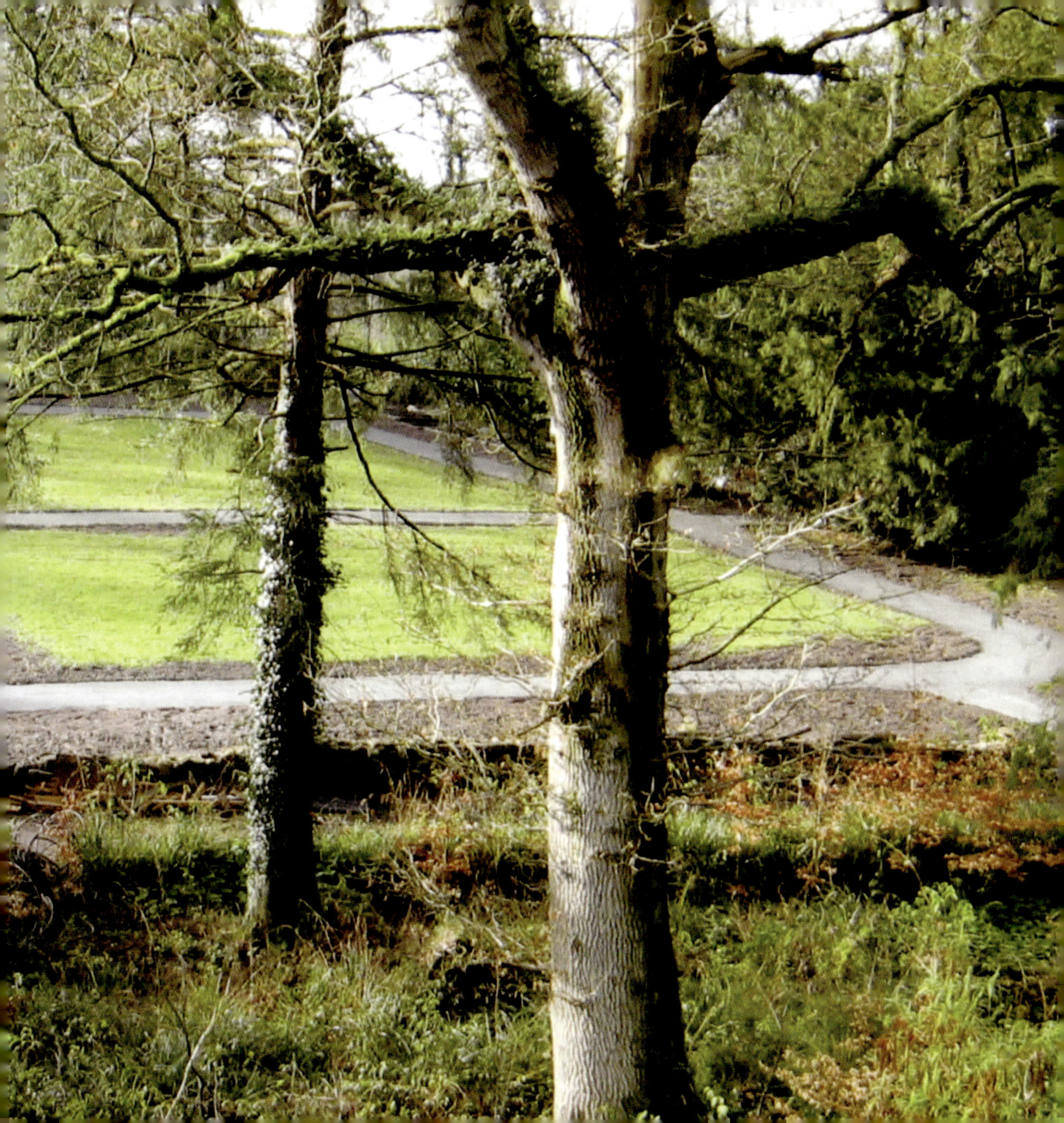

In 2009, an opportunity was provided to restore some features of the estate adjoining the Terrace Garden, which had been identified by the Office of Public Works as areas of special historical interest. The first area to be tackled was the Lady Garden, which is delineated in the Ordnance Survey map of 1840. The garden, associated with Lady Charlotte Barrington, was completely overgrown, with its walls in ruins, when reconstruction work began. Walking in the garden with Sir FitzWilliam Barrington in September 1994, he told me how he remembered the garden in the early 1920s. He recalled a pond in the centre, with a chain pergola around it, and many flower beds from which freshly cut flowers decorated the house every day in the summer. He remembered the bower in which his mother used to sit, in one corner of the garden, and of which some rusty iron remained embedded in a yew tree. The garden formed part of the complex of walks surrounding the castle and he told me that the walk, fringed with bamboo outside the garden, was called the 'bamboonery'. There were two unusual structural

The entrance arch at the west end of the Lady Garden.

features about the garden: firstly, there was a significant slope, south to north, which enabled one to see into the garden from the castle and from the path leading down to it; and, secondly, the two archways in the garden were constructed so that one could see through them to the entrance of the Terrace Garden some hundreds of yards away.

The restoration work was careful to preserve these two features. Once again the 'men of the roads' (the names of Martin, Tony and Gerry come to mind) played a major part in clearing the trees and stone that obscured the line of the original paths. Then it was possible, with a digger, to clear the rubble and relay the paths in their original format with the addition of a path which traversed the fountain in a north/south direction. This work was carried out by Seamus Hayes. Four large lawns were then sown with grass seed by Tom Holmes (Junior) and a new fountain was installed by Eddie Dwyer. A new limestone surround for the fountain was sourced by Fr Philip from Killenaule Stone Quarries. The plan was to have a low maintenance garden and the large

View of the Lady Garden, looking from west to east, before restoration.

The paths and graves inside the Lady Garden before restoration.

View of the Southern wall in the Lady Garden before restoration.

The Eastern wall of the Lady Garden in the early stages of restoration.

The eastern wall of the Lady Garden after the Barrington bench and urns had been placed there.

The restored wall on the south side of the Lady Garden: the work was carried out by Eddie Prodger and Darren Hale (foreground) and by Seamus Hayes (the curved section in the background).

Glenstal Abbey Gardens

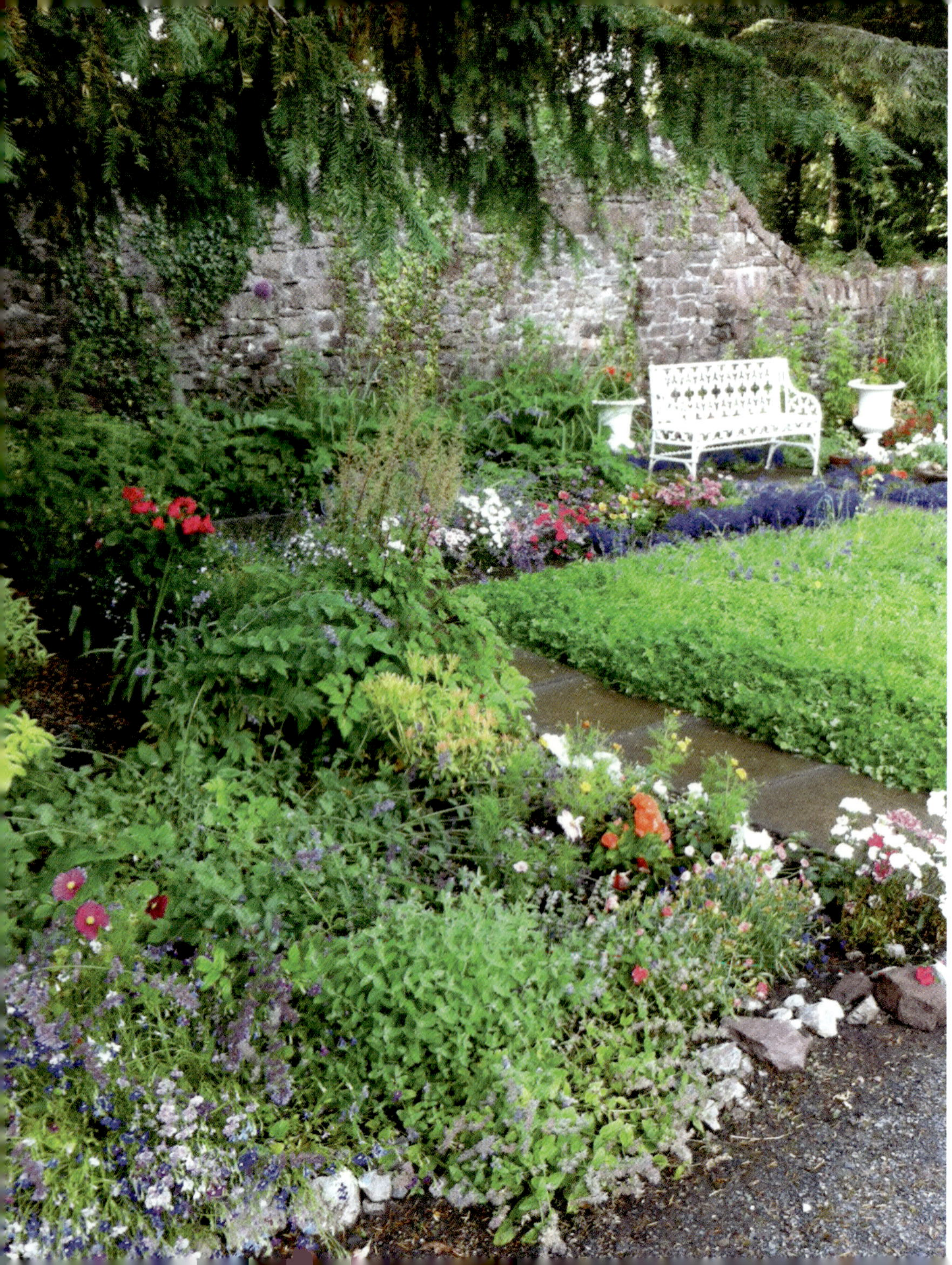

◂ The eastern wall of the Lady Garden fully restored with the planting by Irene Fenton surrounding the Barrington bench.

▴
A view through the two arches of the Lady Garden, which centres on the entrance gate to the Terrace Garden almost 200 metres away. The walls supporting the arches were designed in 1840 to create this remarkable vista.

area of lawn was to be cut by a ride-on mower. Georgie Boyle, a regular member of staff, has carried out this task, and many others, on a regular basis. Other members of staff, notably Paddy O'Connor and Pat Daly, have also provided invaluable help and practical assistance on many occasions. In regard to the Lady Garden, in particular, the entire restoration project was only made possible by the interest and support of Seamus Lantry.

I was mindful, as we completed the work in January 2009, that it was the ninetieth anniversary of the first meeting of Dáil Éireann. I was also aware that the first Dáil had suggested that 16 trees be planted in memory of the 16 men executed at the time of the Easter Rising. With that thought in mind, 16 silver birch trees were planted along one side of the garden and an extra tree was added in memory of Winnie Barrington, who had been accidentally shot in an IRA ambush in 1921. Birch trees were chosen as the work took place in the third month of the ancient Irish Ogham tree calendar (27 December – 23 January) and the

Glenstal Abbey Gardens

birch tree was the tree associated with that month. In the summer of 2012 small memorial stones, carved by Joe Marsh Memorials and giving the basic details of those they commemorated, were placed under the trees. The Cork cultural organisation, Dúnlaoi Teoranta, contributed to the erection of these stones. An account of the planting of these trees, which I wrote for an article in *History Ireland* (March/April 2009), provides a fuller account of the significance of the trees and an unusual Benedictine association with the first plans by Dáil Éireann to undertake such a project in 1919. It reads as follows:

The first meeting of Dáil Éireann (21 January 1919) and the start of the Easter Rising (24 April 1916) have been commemorated in various ways, such as gatherings in the Mansion House, march pasts in the major cities of the state and by a series of lectures and publications. In the course of some recent research on Fr John Sweetman, OSB (1872–1953), I came across an event that provides a fitting opportunity to commemorate both the significance of Dáil Éireann and of the Easter Rising. The minutes of Dáil Éireann, assembled in private session in the Mansion House, 20 August 1919, reveal the plans for an anniversary commemoration that was proposed at that time. The report, presented by Robert Barton (1881–1975), director of agriculture, recommended that 16 trees should be planted in memory of those executed in 1916.

This proposal was made in the context of a programme of afforestation and the holding of a National Arbor Day in the coming month of November. During a short discussion Barton observed that 'as to planting sixteen trees by each farmer, it was a practical suggestion and it appealed to him very much'. The report was approved. The proposal to plant 16 memorial trees, original enough in itself, was made all the more remarkable by the man who made it. Robert Barton had served in the British Army in Dublin in the immediate aftermath of the Easter Rising. As an officer in the Royal Dublin Fusiliers, Barton was placed in charge of the prisoners effects in Richmond Barracks and he also attended some courts martial.

Returning to his landed estate in Annamoe, County Wicklow, in 1918, he was elected as the Sinn Féin representative for West Wicklow in the General Election of that year. He attended the first meeting of Dáil Éireann, 21 January 1919, where he delivered the Dáil's Message to the Free Nations of the World in English.

In the course of the August 1919 Report on Forestry, Seán Etchingham praised Fr John Sweetman for his 'good example' in offering 'eight acres to the Local Sinn Féin Cumann for the purpose of afforestation'. Fr Sweetman was a remarkable man whose life had been transformed by the Easter Rising. Born in Clohamon, County Wexford, he joined the Benedictine abbey at Downside in England and served as a chaplain in the Boer War. Returning to Ireland, he founded a small school at Mount St Benedict's, Gorey, some years before the First World War. He fully supported the war effort and his boys, including the sons of John Dillon, put on a play in the Abbey Theatre to raise funds for wounded soldiers. Following the Easter Rising, Fr Sweetman and two women members of staff, Aileen Keogh and Máire Comerford, dedicated themselves to the ideals of the Irish Republic. As a result of their political conversion, the sons of Thomas Clarke, Countess Markievicz and John MacBride were enrolled in the school. Incidentally, Máire Comerford's book on *The First Dail* (Dublin, 1969) still retains its historical value.

The school was conducted in a highly individual manner: lessons were taught but the regime was Spartan and even eccentric. Erskine Childers who knew Fr Sweetman well, and sometimes stayed at the school, described him as the 'most un-Catholic Catholic' that he had ever met. Fr Sweetman cultivated his own tobacco and produced a Ballyowen brand of cigarettes, which the senior boys were encouraged to smoke. As recalled by Seán MacBride, he also manifested an unusual regard for trees by allowing the boys to cut down one tree for firewood as long they planted six other trees to replace it. With this approach to life, it was no wonder that Fr Sweetman supported the afforestation plans of Dáil Éireann.

The spirit and example of Fr

Sweetman also indirectly played a part in shaping the character of Glenstal School, when Fr Matthew Dillon, a former pupil of his at Gorey, was appointed headmaster in 1937. Fr Matthew brought to his task many of the qualities that he had experienced at Mount St Benedict's. Mindful of Fr Sweetman's connection with Glenstal and the way in which he had supported Dáil Éireann's planting of 16 trees for the men of 1916, it seemed appropriate to give some practical effect to his ideals in the Lady Garden.

On 21 January 2009, therefore, 16 silver birch trees were planted in the spirit of Dáil Éireann's proposal of 1919. They commemorated Patrick Pearse, Thomas Clarke, Thomas MacDonagh (all executed on 3 May); Joseph Plunkett, Edward Daly, Michael O'Hanrahan, William Pearse (all executed on 4 May); John McBride (executed 5 May); Con Colbert, Edmund Kent, Michael Mallin, Sean Heuston (all executed on 8 May); Thomas Kent (executed 9 May); James Connolly, Seán MacDermott (both executed on 12 May) and Roger Casement (executed 3 August). One extra tree was also planted. This tree was planted in memory of Winnie Barrington, aged 23, who was killed in an IRA ambush at Coolboreen Bridge, Newport, County Tipperary, on 14 May 1921. The ambush was directed against Inspector Henry Biggs, RIC, who was also killed, but Winnie was travelling with him in his car. As well as marking the death of an innocent victim of war, the tree may also serve as a reminder of the enduring good will of the Barrington family towards the local community and of their own great love of trees. Fortunately, some of the trees which they planted remain in the estate and surround the walls of the garden where Winnie's silver birch is planted. The words on her tomb stone, in nearby Abington Cemetery, provide hopeful, if mysterious, inspiration for all those who commemorate their dead in any way. The words read: 'here lies buried all that could die of Winnie Barrington'. A poem by John Liddy conveys the ideals and sentiments which inspired the planting of these silver birch trees.

The postcard, addressed to Mike Hayes, Moher, Murroe, and sent from the Hôtel du Parc, Cannes, Alpes-Maritimes, France, reads as follows: 'I hope you are all grand and best wishes for 1921. It is very hot out here and lovely scenery but I am looking forward tremendously to returning to Ireland in March. I have been to a few dances and plays, one Irish one was grand. I'll ride up and see you directly I get home. Best regards to you all and to Fr John, W.F. Barrington.'

The postcard was dated 16 January 1921. The fact that Mike Hayes was publicly known to be a member of the IRA sheds new light on the life and death of Winnie Barrington. But that is part of another story.

Winifred (Winnie) Barrington (5 July 1897 – 14 May 1921) was the first child of Sir Charles and Lady Mary Rose Barrington. She attended Cheltenham Ladies College and served as a volunteer nurse, working with wounded soldiers, in England during the First World War

Glenstal Abbey Gardens

The Silver Birch

'Symbol of the first Dáil and the 1916 executions,
It provided axe handles, cradles and pain relief
From its inner bark, a cure for arthritis in its leaves.

Men and schoolboys were birched to the bone
By it but new beginnings and opportunities wave to us
Because Fr Brian, in the third month of Ogham

Tree calendar gave voice to its first consonant B
By planting seventeen silver birches in Charlotte
Barrington's Glenstal garden; one for Winnie.

Her loss was grief amongst Murroe locals
When killed at Coolboreen in a 1921 IRA ambush
Along with their target Inspector Biggs.

That such a tree could be singled out to stand
For so much is proof of its enduring esteem.
May it sway firm against the fiercest wind,
Rejuvenate with its power of healing.'

John Liddy, 2012

The restoration work on the Lady Garden continued after the paths were relaid. All the walls were in urgent need of attention and repairs began immediately: Eddie Prodger, again assisted by his son and Darren Hale, repaired a large section of one wall and created two stone piers at the side entrance. Seamus Hayes carried out major renewal and restoration work on the other walls. In the course of the work, a small dwelling space was uncovered on the western side of the garden wall near the monastery graveyard. This area is a favourite spot for the red squirrels as they move along the wall and jump into the surrounding trees. One small corner of the garden was laid out with paths, flowers and seating, which was provided by bringing the Barrington wrought-iron bench from its former place in the Terrace Garden. At the time of writing, a new lawn has been laid in front of the bench and a wide variety of flowers, planted and tended by the regular efforts of Irene Fenton, provide an attractive vista. She has also made more attractive the area surrounding the graves inside the Lady Garden.

A view of some of the newly planted silver birch trees and restored garden wall behind gravestones.

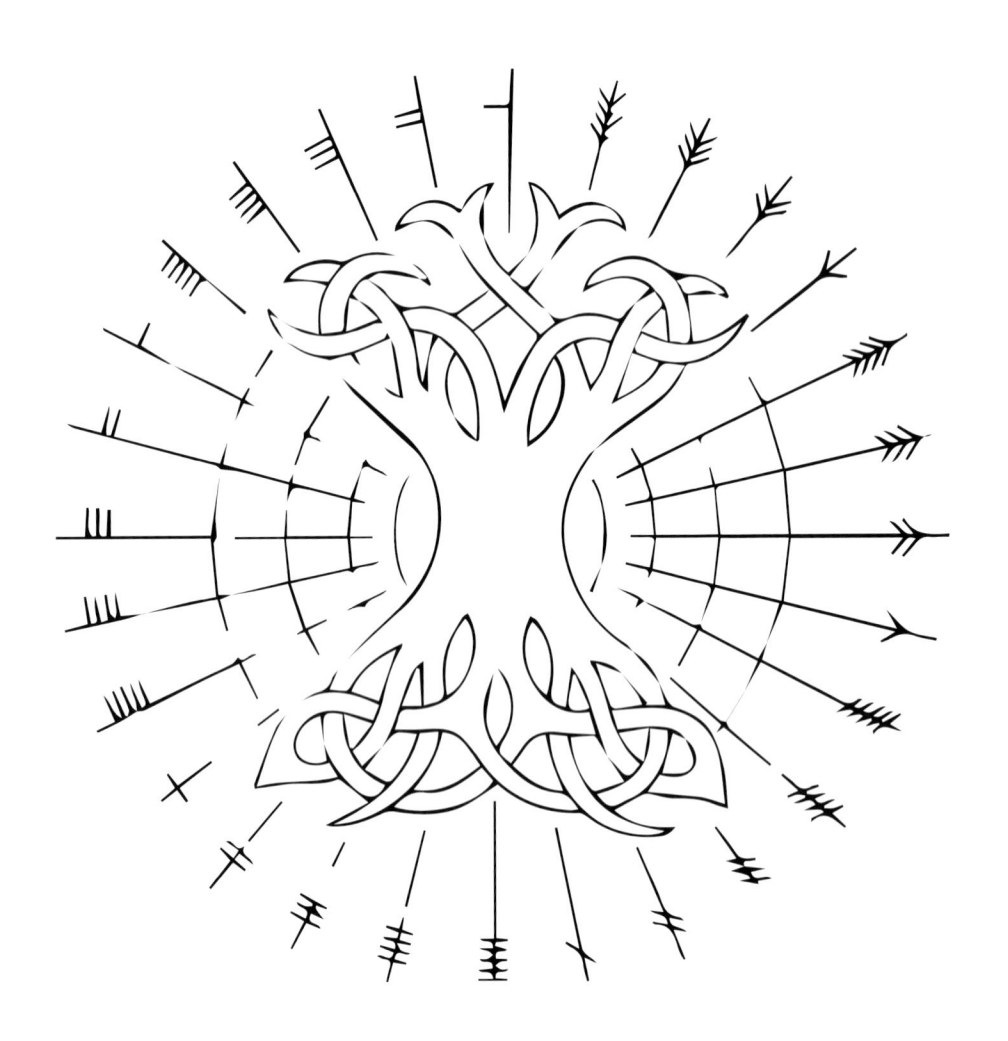

The Planting of the Ogham Tree Calendar

While the basic maintenance work has continued, two initiatives were taken: firstly, work was carried out on the ruins immediately outside the garden; and, secondly, a special planting of trees was undertaken in the upper orchard field. The ruins to the east of the garden and immediately above the glen are marked on the Ordnance Survey map of 1840. I was aware of them not only from the map but also from seeing their outline in the glen outside the top gate of the garden. At the end of April 2012, we (Br Jacob, Seamus Hayes and myself) began a careful dig of the area and the clearance of some sheds. Many trees that had been planted inside the curtilage of the ruins were removed. The clearance revealed substantial remains overlooking the glen. An informal visit from two archaeologists in mid-June indicated that the ruins predated the Barrington buildings on the side of the garden (the bothies or outhouses) and might well date back to the 1600s or earlier. Further investigation is required but, at present, it appears that the ruins may possibly go back to the time of the Mulryan Castle of *c.* 1400. The site is not only of historical interest but also offers spectacular views of the glen.

The tree planting in the upper orchard field took place at the end of May. I had seen a walkway of trees dedicated to the trees of the ancient Ogham alphabet in the grounds of the Castletroy Hotel in Limerick and I decided to adapt it. The concept was interesting and it offered attractive design possibilities. The Ogham alphabet is of Celtic origin and is based on the lunar calendar year. For each month of the year, and there are 13 months, a tree is chosen and a letter of the alphabet is also associated with the tree. As there are two yew trees inside the top terrace of the garden, I decided that they would form the start of the tree calendar. Then, in the walled enclosure above, the other trees were planted, in groups of threes and in a circular fashion. There is some debate about the structure of the calendar and the planting was based on the book by Niall MacCoitir, *Irish Trees. Myths, Legends and Folklore* (Cork, 2003). For the record, it might be of interest to list them:

first month, (1 Nov. to 28 Nov.) the yew tree, letter I;

second month (29 Nov. to 26 Dec.) the pine tree, letter A;

third month (27 Dec. to 23 Jan.) the birch tree, letter B;

fourth month (24 Jan. to 20 Feb.) the rowan tree, letter L;

fifth month (21 Feb. to 20 Mar.) the alder tree, letter F;

sixth month (21 Mar. to 17 Apr.) the willow tree, letter S;

seventh month (18 Apr. to 15 May) the hawthorn, letter H;

eighth month (16 May to 12 Jun.) the ash tree, letter O;

ninth month (13 Jun. to 10 Jul.) the oak tree, letter D;

tenth month (11 Jul. to 7 Aug.) the holly tree, letter T;

eleventh month (8 Aug. to 4 Sept.) the hazel tree, letter C;

twelfth month (5 Sept. to 2 Oct.) the apple tree, letter Q;

thirteenth month (3 Oct. to 30 Oct.) the elder tree, letter R.

Other trees, not included in the tree calendar, complete the Ogham alphabet. The trees that were planted were young trees of Irish origin and were sourced from Stephen Powell of the Limerick market. Thanks to the endeavours of Tom Holmes and Seamus Hayes, the planting was completed in early June and benefitted from our unusually wet summer — the wettest June on record. The work was made possible by the interest and help of Irene Fenton. Rain has been the dominant influence on gardening during this current year. So much so that one is tempted to adjust the traditional verse on the value of the garden, as follows:

The soft drops of rain for pardon,
The song of the birds for mirth.
One is closer to God in a garden,
Than anywhere else on earth.

Despite the rain, the lines of the gardens retain their restored look, although, partly out of necessity and partly out of choice, the planting has, in many places, the look of a wildlife garden. Having regard to the preservation of frogs, the area given over to native Irish grasses has increased. They also appear in some of the beds in the Bible Garden. There is a certain rationale behind this development. Over the years one learns that plants and grasses know what is best for themselves and I have developed a pattern for planting. It is based on, what I call, the five Ss plus C principle! That is to say one takes into account the following: Soil, Size, Shape, Season, Scent and Colour. Here I am encouraged by the advice of Jesus, which I have mentioned above, that we should be like the flowers of the field: do not be anxious about tomorrow, do not be stressed, do not work too hard (or words to that effect!) With those thoughts in mind, the words of Psalm 64 may be selected to convey some impression of God's presence in the small patches of land that we call gardens and of the efforts of many people, over hundreds of years, to transform townlands into a Terrace Garden and beyond:

The lands of sunrise and sunset,
you fill with your joy.
You care for the earth, give it water,
you fill it with riches.
Your river in heaven brims over to provide its grain.
And thus you provide for the earth;
you drench its furrows,
You level it, soften it with showers,
you bless its growth.
You crown the year with your goodness,
abundance flows in your steps,
In the pastures of the wilderness it flows.
The hills are girded with joy,
the meadows covered with flocks.
The valleys are decked with wheat.
They shout for joy, yes, they sing.

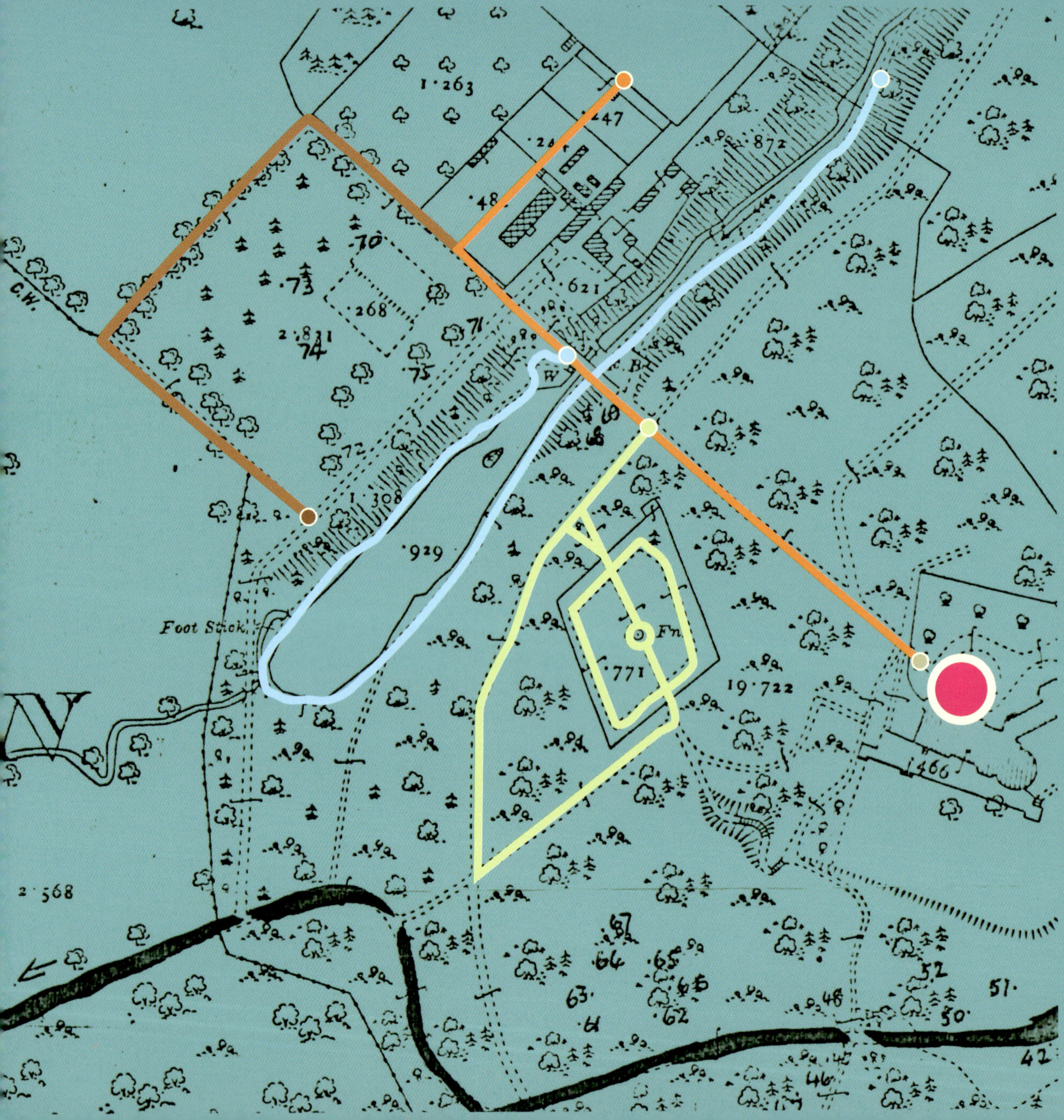

1·263
247
872
48
70
73
268
621
2·811
74
71
75
W
B
68
72
1·308
929
Foot Stick
Fn
771
19·722
466
2·568
67
64
65
63
62
48
52
51
50
42
46

Outline of the Garden Walks Mentioned in the Book

- Deer Park Walk
- Walk To The Terrace Garden
- Chapel Lake and Mass Rock Walk
- Entrance & Reception
- Lady Garden Walk
- Main Road

PAPAVER EDITIONS